ORGANIZING
AMAZON

ORGANIZING AMAZON

Building Worker Power under
Conditions of Fragmentation,
Precarity and Regimentation

Tom Vickers

with essays by Rachel Fagan,
Amanda Gearing, Garfield Hylton,
Louveza Iqbal, Ceferina Floresca Javier,
Paramanathan Pradeep, Stuart Richards,
Tom Rigby and Ferdousara Uddin

B BRISTOL
UNIVERSITY
PRESS

First published in Great Britain in 2025 by

Bristol University Press
University of Bristol
1–9 Old Park Hill
Bristol
BS2 8BB
UK
t: +44 (0)117 374 6645
e: bup-info@bristol.ac.uk

Details of international sales and distribution partners are available at
bristoluniversitypress.co.uk

British Library Cataloguing in Publication Data
A catalogue record for this book is available from the British Library

ISBN 978-1-5292-5429-7 paperback
ISBN 978-1-5292-5430-3 ePub
ISBN 978-1-5292-5431-0 ePdf

Cover design: Nicky Borowiec
Front cover image: Luke Boucher via GMB Union
Bristol University Press uses environmentally responsible
print partners.
Printed and bound in Great Britain by CPI Group (UK) Ltd,
Croydon, CR0 4YY

Bristol University Press' authorised representative in the
European Union is: Easy Access System Europe,
Mustamäe tee 50, 10621 Tallinn, Estonia,
Email: gpsr.requests@easproject.com

FSC
www.fsc.org
MIX
Paper | Supporting
responsible forestry
FSC® C013604

Contents

About the Author and Contributors

Tom Vickers is Associate Professor of Sociology at Nottingham Trent University, UK, and Director of the GMB–NTU Work Futures Observatory.

Garfield Hylton, **Louveza Iqbal**, **Ceferina Floresca Javier** and **Paramanathan Pradeep** are GMB worker-leaders at Amazon BHX4.

Rachel Fagan, **Amanda Gearing**, **Stuart Richards**, **Tom Rigby** and **Ferdousara Uddin** are officers in the GMB Midlands region.

Acknowledgements

Thanks are due to: the Amazon workers and GMB worker-leaders and organizers who trusted me with their stories and allowed me to move in their spaces; Nottingham Trent University for funding my secondment to the GMB and for co-funding, with the GMB, the Work Futures Observatory, which enabled the research that forms the basis for this book; Michael Whittall and Jereme Snook, who helped to articulate the book's theoretical framework; Dominic Holland and David Dahill, whose research helped lay the foundations for my collaboration with the GMB; Dr Jennifer Allsopp, without whose constant support this book would not have been written and whose *Dante on the Move* anthology and introduction to the work of Brian Dillon gave me the idea to include essays by worker-leaders and organizers as part of this book; the anonymous peer reviewers and editors at Bristol University Press, whose feedback considerably strengthened this book; and my children Ellen and Rowan, who inspire me every day to try to be a better person and to fight for a better world.

1

Introduction

This book examines the extraordinarily rapid unionization of Amazon's BHX4 warehouse in Coventry, England, between August 2022 and July 2024. Over this period, membership of the GMB Union grew from around 60 to over 1,400, 37 days of official strike action took place and workers achieved a combined pay rise of 28.5 per cent, greater than any other country in Amazon Europe. Yet in July 2024, the union narrowly lost a ballot of the workforce – by just 28 votes on an 86 per cent turnout – that would have forced the company to recognize the union and enter into formal negotiations. This book provides a detailed assessment of the union's practice during this campaign and the critical factors leading to its successes and defeats. It draws on an intensive period of ethnographic research between January and July 2024, interspersed with personal essays by worker-leaders and organizers who were directly involved. The intensity of this struggle brings into stark relief underlying features of labour relations and union strategy that may be harder to detect in other contexts. This is used to systematize a distinctive organizing model that has widespread relevance, as a form of 'middle range' theory that is well suited to understanding the outcomes in particular workplaces.[1]

Key insights for trade unionists, workers and organizers include: practical strategies and tactics to reach the workforce (Chapter 3), sustain engagement (Chapter 4), develop leadership (Chapter 5), respond to workers' needs (Chapter 6) and build wider support (Chapter 7), and a coherent framework to bring these elements together into a coherent model (Chapter 8) that creates space and time for organizing, even where an employer operates a tight regime of control and opposes union access. It also offers insights for organizing workers who are precarious and fragmented by the structures of the workplace or differences of language, nationality or immigration status, demonstrating that challenges to access extend far beyond formal rights.

Key insights for scholars and students include: a detailed case study that challenges the idea that 'traditional' trade unions like the GMB are poorly suited to organizing diverse, precarious workforces.[2] Amazon's global reach – with warehouses on every continent apart from Antarctica – and its leading market position add to the importance of these findings for the future of industrial relations, work and employment. While there is a growing literature on Amazon, much of this is journalistic. Academic texts provide a wealth of important insights,[3] but their main focus is on the organization and management of labour, and they do not discuss trade union strategies or practice in great detail. This book contributes to filling that gap, adding to knowledge of the latest developments in the 'organizing turn',[4] and trade union adaptation to the changing composition of the working class and labour practices.[5] Questions to assist in using this as a case study for teaching are included as Appendix 1.

Coventry is a city with a strong history of working–class organization, particularly within the automotive industry, but has faced decades of deindustrialization that have hollowed out that working class power.[6] Amazon is typical of low-waged and insecure warehousing jobs that are now prevalent in and around the city, attracted by Coventry's central location within the UK and proximity to major road links and the Birmingham (BHX) Airport. BHX4 has strategic importance for Amazon as one of only two 'cross-dock' warehouses in the company's UK network, which break down bulk shipments to be distributed to 31 fulfilment centres.

The next part of this chapter situates the organizing process at BHX4 within the international context of efforts to unionize Amazon. It then presents the book's theoretical approach and concludes with an outline of the remainder of the volume. The methodology is provided as Appendix 2.

Organizing Amazon

A growing international literature shows that Amazon is consistently determined to resist unionization and is willing to spend considerable resources to this end.[7] A very early attempt was made in 2002 to unionize an Amazon UK warehouse in Milton Keynes, just eight years after the company was founded and three years after it began operating in the UK. After the British Graphical, Paper and Media Union (since merged with Unite the Union) signed up over 10 per cent of the workforce, the Central Arbitration Committee (CAC), which oversees union recognition in the UK, granted a ballot to assess whether there was majority support for the union within that warehouse. This is the key test under UK rules before the CAC will force a company to recognize a union and commence formal bargaining. Following a campaign by the company that included several wage increases, dismissals of leading union members and extensive anti-union agitation on the shop floor, union recognition was rejected by 80 per cent of voters on a 90 per cent turnout.[8]

Amazon claims that it respects its employees' right to join a union, and that it provides structures for workers (or 'Associates' in Amazon's terminology) to express their views – including a 'Voice of the Associates' (VOA) digital message board and a delegate 'Associate Forum'. Fairwork assesses these claims and concludes that the VOA Board and Associate Forum are 'not meaningfully independent of management'[9] and as such do not constitute fair representation. Fairwork also reviews the extensive evidence of Amazon's anti-union practices, echoing the findings of Delfanti.[10] Delfanti argues that these practices are not an arbitrary feature of Amazon's management, but arise from the company's commitment to 'frictionless' movement of commodities by all means necessary, in which 'Workers are the most problematic factor ... and must be carefully controlled and governed', lest they slow down this process.[11] Amazon's explicitly anti-union measures combine with features of the workplace that systematically undermine collectivization:

> Amazon has used years of workplace data and designed its warehouses and workplaces specifically to be difficult to organise. They have high turnover and workforces who are insecure and have no job security ... staggered breaks and shift changes, which makes it difficult for large numbers of workers to talk to one another ... [and] workforces are split by race, gender, or national origin.[12]

3

In spite of this, and perhaps partly in response to the company's tight regime of control, there have been important periods of unionization at Amazon sites in many countries, often involving strike action.[13] In Europe this includes Germany from 2013, France from 2014, Poland from 2015, Italy from 2017 and Spain from 2018. Other acts of resistance by Amazon workers, some involving formal trade unions and some organized informally, have included petitions, protests and temporary work stoppages or slowdowns.[14]

While national legislative, regulatory and political differences have affected the course that unionization has taken in different countries, the centralization of Amazon's management and operational design leads Delfanti to argue that Amazon workers' 'experiences are generalizable in a way that might not be true of other companies'.[15] Such widespread worker activism across many different countries demonstrates that there must be similarly widespread features of Amazon's work process that push people to take action. And, indeed, transnational as well as national organizing among Amazon workers continues to grow.[16] Yet, despite these conditions and repeated actions, unions have frequently found it difficult to organize a large proportion of the workforce.[17] This underscores the challenges of organizing Amazon workers and the significance of the GMB's rapid and sustained recruitment at BHX4, which calls for a detailed study.

Theoretical framework: time, space and mobility-as-labour

This book's analysis is informed by an understanding of labour as a contested movement of the human body through time and space.[18] This begins from the observation that labour hinges on the mobility of the human body – in other words, its capacity for movement, which can be put to various uses. As Marx notes, labour involves 'setting in motion arms and legs, head and hands, the natural forces of his body, in order to appropriate nature's productions in a form adapted to his own wants'.[19] Under capitalism, wage labourers are not free to direct the motion of their bodies directly towards their own needs, but are compelled to direct them towards the demands of their employer, who uses only a part of the value produced to pay workers enough to ensure they continue working, taking the rest as profit. How to bend workers to these ends and the consequences for the worker and the employer are far from simple. By signing an employment contract, a worker may agree to appear at a designated place (the workplace) and remain there for a specific period of time (the working day). Nevertheless, contracts are often less specific when it comes to their bodily motion within that time and place. An employer might direct a worker to nail two pieces of wood together as part of a labour process leading to the production of a table. Yet, how many strikes of the hammer does this require? How many pieces of wood can a worker join in an hour? Does the stress of wielding a hammer impact efficiency towards the end of the working day? And how does this activity, directed towards the employer's needs, affect the wellbeing of the worker, as they repeat this activity over months and years?

The mobile activity of workers, and the means to which this is put in the labour process, thus affects both the profitability of the worker for the employer and the demands that are placed on the worker's body and mind, directly impacting their wellbeing, which in turn affects their capacity for work in the future. The picture is further complicated when we acknowledge that human bodies are raced, gendered and marked in other ways that play a significant role in the selection, management and reward of labour.[20] Answering these questions in a particular workplace requires attention to both the power relations between the buyer and seller of labour power and the subjective perspectives of workers. Trade unions can affect both, with tremendous capacity to help workers assert their needs within the labour process and also to play an educational role that affects how workers perceive their work, the potential power they wield, and their relationships with other workers and the employer.

Human mobility can be measured using time and space, both of which can be understood relationally – time representing a sequential relation between the same thing and space representing a parallel relation between multiple things. As E.P. Thompson demonstrates, capitalism has given rise to a commodification of time, centred around managing the motions of labour.[21] The same may be said of space. Mezzadra and Neilson argue that this commodification has proceeded, up to the present day, to colonize more and more of the total time and space of life.[22] We see this, for example, in zero-hours contracts that require workers to set aside much more of their time than they actually work or are paid for in order to be available when called, expectations that workers engage in self-education for work or deal with work communications outside paid hours, or, as at Amazon, the habitual reliance on overtime that pushes many workers to work 60 hours per week.

Yet, because human labour is inseparable from living human bodies that possess agency, the commodification of time and space is perpetually incomplete. As Hyman's sociological analysis of power relations and conflict between employers and workers suggests, the subjective and structural issues at play result in a transaction that remains inconclusive and transitory.[23] This helps to explain capital's dependency on managerial hierarchies, which represent mechanisms that attempt to control the commodification of time and space. Wage rates may seem separate from such questions of mobility within the labour process, and yet they influence such temporal and spatial issues as how many hours an individual must work, moving according to the employer's demands in order to earn enough money to meet their needs, as well as the distance they must travel from their place of work to find housing they can afford, and their ability to accumulate savings as a buffer against the threat of unemployment as the employer's last resort against workers who resist their demands.

Centring this inherent contest over the commodification of time and space, and the dynamic movement of labouring bodies that this seeks to manage, highlights the persistent possibilities for conflict as workers assert their own wants and needs. 'Mobility power' conceptualizes the ability for people to exercise control over their movement, including its form, direction and speed, offering potential for resistance to the demands of employers, and a way of asserting agency over one's labour power.[24] Yet, further complicating matters, we cannot assume a necessary correspondence between worker agency and work practices that support workers' wellbeing; as I have previously shown,[25] workers can have many reasons for choosing to accept precarious and sometimes harmful working conditions.[26]

Applying this theoretical framework to Amazon, as will be explored further later on, we see forms of mobility-as-labour that are highly regimented, with workers' performance digitally monitored against algorithmically determined target rates for speed and quality.[27] A worker's performance against these targets is not disclosed to them until it becomes grounds for disciplinary action, by which time it is already too late. This breeds a perpetual fear for each worker that they might be working too slowly and thereby become subject to discipline.

Across the warehouse, workers' movements are fragmented along multiple lines, including narrowly defined and widely varying tasks and roles, divisions into departments and shifts that restrict opportunities for contact, and an array of nationalities and languages among workers with little opportunity for social mixing. All of this is underpinned by states of precarity that for many involve little job security, in some cases variable hours, limited time to build support networks outside of work, and for some workers restricted rights due to their immigration status.

Such circumstances leave precarious workers off-balance, making it difficult to plan or strategize,[28] and therefore in a poor position to assert their needs or attempt to exercise control over their movements. This is the context in which BHX4 workers and GMB organizers found ways to unionize, representing a radically different form of movement, in which each key step in the collective dance was decided together democratically, seeking harmony with workers' needs against the demands of the employer. In doing so, GMB workers and organizers produced important lessons for how to challenge the profit-centred mobility logic of companies like Amazon.

Structure of the book

Chapter 2 introduces the GMB Union through a discussion of some key moments in its history, followed by a discussion of organizing concepts that informed the union's work at BHX4 and its relationship with the organizing literature.

Chapters 3–7 are organized around the five areas of challenge that were identified as shaping the unionization process at BHX4. Each of these chapters begins with an overview of the principal challenge that forms the focus of that chapter, before presenting the GMB's response, followed by a discussion of the wider implications for employment and trade union organizing. At the end of each of these chapters, questions are offered to readers who are involved in organizing themselves, as prompts to invite reflection on the reader's own practice. These chapters are organized as follows:

- Chapter 3 addresses the challenges involved in reaching the whole workforce and the GMB's response, from laying the groundwork through a slow process of casework and advocacy, to seizing the moment when unofficial 'wildcat' protests erupted in 2022, to the use of official strikes to create a space and time in which workers could more freely associate.
- Chapter 4 considers the challenges that made it difficult to sustain action and engagement and the GMB's responses, including a substantial strike fund, new practices to win strike ballots, and the application for statutory union recognition.
- Chapter 5 discusses the systematic approach to building leadership across a highly divided and controlled workforce, from the methods organizers used to identify organic leaders without having access to the workplace to the weekly leadership development sessions and mentoring.
- Chapter 6 explores how the GMB responded to workers' needs, accounting for the many different issues members faced and the impact of circumstances outside of the workplace, from health problems to housing, family and visa concerns.
- Chapter 7 reflects on steps the GMB took to build wider support for the BHX4 workers, including the Amazon Workers Support Group, specialist support and resources from the Trades Union Congress (TUC), nongovernmental organizations (NGOs) such as Foxglove and Brushstrokes, and academic researchers.

Chapter 8 presents six core principles that constitute the Coventry Model, derived from the analytical process described earlier in this chapter:

1. *Capitalize* on spontaneous ruptures in the employer's control.
2. *Create* democratic spaces and times outside the employers' control.
3. *Cultivate* worker leadership through deep support and education.
4. *Connect* with workers' lives beyond the workplace.
5. *Challenge* the employer's freedom to operate.
6. *Contest* employer control of the workplace.

Chapter 9 concludes with reflections on the further development of the Coventry Model, the wider implications for work and trade unionism, and the contribution of these findings to understanding struggles for mobility power.

Notes

[1] Doellgast, V., Bidwell, M. and Colvin, A.J.S. (2021) 'New directions in employment relations theory: understanding fragmentation, identity, and legitimacy', *ILR Review*, 74(3): 555–579.

[2] Però, D. (2020) 'Indie unions, organising and labour renewal: learning from precarious migrant workers', *Work, Employment and Society*, 34(5): 900–918; Bailey, D.J. (2024) 'Worker-led dissent in the age of austerity: comparing the conditions of success', *Work, Employment and Society*, 38(4): 1041–1061.

[3] See, for example, Alimahomed-Wilson, J. and Reese, E. (eds) (2020) *The Cost of Free Shipping: Amazon in the Global Economy*, London: Pluto Press; Delfanti, A. (2021) *The Warehouse: Workers and Robots at Amazon*, London: Pluto Press; Vallas, S.P. and Kronberg, A.-K. (2023) 'Coercion, consent, and class consciousness: how workers respond to Amazon's production regime', *Socius*, 9, DOI:10.1177/23780231231216286; Kassem, S. (2023) *Work and Alienation in the Platform Economy: Amazon and the Power of Organisation*, Bristol: Bristol University Press.

[4] Holgate, J. (2021) *Arise: Power, Strategy and Union Resurgence*, London: Pluto Press.

[5] Johnson, M. and Herman, E. (2024) 'Out with the old, in with the new? Institutional experimentation and decent work in the UK', *Economic and Industrial Democracy*, DOI:10.1177/0143831X231220528.

[6] Blissett, E. (2023) 'British trade unionism in the 1980s reassessed: Are recurring assumptions about union membership and strikes flawed?', *Labor History*, 64(5): 547–574.

[7] Kassem (n 3).

[8] Boewe, J. and Schulten, J. (2020) 'Amazon strikes in Europe: seven years of industrial action, challenges, and strategies', in J. Alimahomed-Wilson and E. Reese (eds) *The Cost of Free Shipping: Amazon in the Global Economy*, London: Pluto Press, pp 209–224.

[9] Fairwork (2024) 'Fairwork Amazon Report 2024: Transformation of the warehouse sector through AI'. Report, Global Partnership on AI, p 18.

[10] Delfanti (n 3).

[11] Delfanti (n 3), p 9.

[12] Kaoosji, S. (2020) 'Worker and community organising to challenge Amazon's algorithmic threat', in J. Alimahomed-Wilson and E. Reese

(eds) *The Cost of Free Shipping: Amazon in the Global Economy*, London: Pluto Press, pp 194–205, at p 201.

[13] Massimo, F. (2020) 'A struggle for bodies and souls: Amazon management and union strategies in France and Italy, in J. Alimahomed-Wilson and E. Reese (eds) *The Cost of Free Shipping: Amazon in the Global Economy*, London: Pluto Press, pp 129–144.

[14] For specific examples, see Holland, D. and Vickers, T. (2021) 'Unfulfilled? Evidence review on work, labour and employment in Amazon's fulfilment centres'. Report, Nottingham Trent University.

[15] Delfanti (n 3), p 6.

[16] Kassem (n 3).

[17] Alimahomed-Wilson and Reese (n 3).

[18] This is presented in more detail in Vickers, T. (2019) *Borders, Migration and Class: Producing Immigrants and Workers*, Bristol: Bristol University Press.

[19] Marx, K. (1887/2010) *Capital, Volume 1*, Moscow: Progress Publishers/Marxist Internet Archive, ch 7, s 1.

[20] Mezzadra, S. and Neilson, B. (2013) *Border as Method, or, The Multiplication of Labour*, Durham, NC: Duke University Press.

[21] Thompson, E.P. (1967) 'Time, work-discipline, and industrial capitalism', *Past & Present*, 38: 56–97.

[22] Mezzadra and Neilson (n 20).

[23] Hyman, R. (1989). *Strikes*, London: Macmillan.

[24] Alberti, G. (2014) 'Mobility strategies, "mobility differentials" and "transnational exit": the experiences of precarious migrants in London's hospitality jobs', *Work, Employment and Society*, 28(6): 865–881; Vickers (n 18).

[25] Vickers (n 18).

[26] See also Alberti (n 24); Waite, L., Craig, G., Lewis, H., and Skrivankova, K. (eds) (2015) *Vulnerability, Exploitation and Migrants: Insecure Work in a Globalised Economy*, London: Palgrave Macmillan.

[27] For further details, see Delfanti (n 3); Kassem (n 3); Fairwork (n 9).

[28] Datta, K., McIlwaine, C., Evans, Y., Herbert, J., May, J., and Wills, J. (2007) 'From coping strategies to tactics: London's low-pay economy and migrant labour', *British Journal of Industrial Relations*, 45(2): 404–432.

ESSAY 1

What We Have Achieved Is Not a List of Accomplishments, It's a Transformation

Ceferina Floresca Javier, GMB worker-leader at BHX4 and recipient of the GMB's Eleanor Marx Award

The story of Amazon BHX4 in Coventry is not one of quick victories or a tidy list of achievements. It's a story of transformation – a deep, ongoing change that reflects the heart and resilience of the workers who have pushed back against a behemoth that thrives on efficiency and control. What we've accomplished so far isn't just a tally of successful actions, negotiations or strikes, but rather the creation of a movement, a culture shift, and a collective sense of identity and power that simply did not exist before. At its core, this is a transformation of people and place.

To understand what we're fighting for, we need to start by painting a picture of life inside the warehouse. For most workers, it's a world of constant movement and relentless pressure, where your performance is measured by algorithms and your breaks are timed down to the second. The physical and mental demands of working in this environment take a toll, and many of us felt that we were seen not as people, but as units of labour to be pushed to the limit.

Despite this, Amazon Coventry represents more than just a place of work. It is home to thousands of workers who live in the surrounding communities, people with families, dreams, and aspirations for a better life. Yet for so long, those of us working in this facility felt disempowered, isolated and unable to change the conditions we faced daily. It's here where the seed of transformation began to grow.

The first rumblings of discontent were not just about wages or breaks, although those were important issues. They were about dignity, respect and the feeling that we deserved a voice in decisions that impacted our lives. Amazon had long maintained a strict anti-union stance, and any talk of unionization was swiftly countered with internal propaganda campaigns, team meetings with management and thinly veiled threats about what joining a union could mean for our jobs.

But despite this, something changed. The pandemic revealed the fragility of Amazon's workforce model – workers were essential to keeping the economy going, yet we were being treated as disposable. During this time, workers started to talk, organize and imagine what could happen if we stood up for ourselves. With the support of the GMB Union, conversations turned into action, and we began to see what might be possible if we united.

This was not an overnight transformation. Many of us had never been part of a union, and the idea of going up against Amazon felt intimidating. Yet the movement began to grow. Our colleagues who had once been silent started to raise their voices, and we began to form a collective identity – a community of workers who believed in something bigger than just ourselves.

One of the most pivotal moments in our journey was the recognition ballot in July 2024, a crucial step in our quest to be officially recognized by Amazon. This recognition would have given us the right to negotiate collectively on behalf of all workers in the warehouse, a powerful tool in shaping the conditions under which we work.

Unfortunately, despite our best efforts, we lost the recognition ballot by 28 votes. It was a bitter pill to swallow, especially as we were well aware of the lengths Amazon had gone to in order to prevent us from organizing. They held meetings to sow fear and uncertainty, and used every tactic at their disposal to disrupt our campaign. It was a tough defeat, but it was not the end.

What happened next is the true testament to our transformation. Rather than being defeated, we became more determined. The loss of the ballot didn't destroy our movement; it deepened our resolve. We knew that this was not just a fight for better pay or working conditions – this was a fight for our rights, for our ability to be heard and for the respect we deserved as human beings.

We've built a community, a culture of solidarity that is stronger than any of the anti-union tactics that Amazon can throw at us. However, the most important transformation is the one that has taken place within us. Many of us who had never before imagined ourselves as part of a union now proudly wear that label. People who once stayed silent during workplace disputes are now standing up for their rights and the rights of their colleagues. The confidence that has grown from this collective action is something that cannot be taken away, regardless of Amazon's opposition.

While we've made significant progress, we know that this is just the beginning. We are reaching out to more workers, building stronger relationships and expanding our base of support within the warehouse and beyond. Workers in other Amazon facilities across the UK have been watching our fight closely, and many have been inspired to start their own organizing efforts.

We also know that our fight is not just about what happens at Amazon Coventry; it's part of a larger movement of workers around the world who are standing up to corporations that prioritize profit over people. The transformation we've undergone is not unique – it's part of a global shift towards workers reclaiming their power and demanding that their voices be heard. We've faced setbacks and will likely face more, but the important thing is that we now know our strength. And that is something Amazon can never take away.

2

Introducing the GMB Union

This chapter reviews important periods in the GMB's history in
order to give context to the union's recent work at BHX4. Given the
highly international character of the workforce at BHX4, particular
attention is given to the GMB's record of responding to the needs
of workers with a migrant background, and the closely related issues
of race and racism. Consistent with the GMB's own practice, this
book uses 'Global Majority' to refer to workers of African, Asian
or Latin-American descent. This is followed by a discussion of the
GMB's organizing strategy at BHX4, set in the context of relevant
parts of the literature on organizing.

The GMB is the third-largest trade union in the UK, with more
than half a million members, and its origins date back to the Gas
Workers and General Union founded in 1889.[1] Its rapid success in
building its membership among the highly diverse and precarious
workforce at BHX4 contradicts a widely held idea that Britain's large,
formalized trade unions are poorly suited to grassroots organizing
and tend to seek class compromise in defence of a labour elite,[2] in
contrast to the agile militancy of smaller 'indie' trade unions.[3] Some
writers have suggested that traditional unions like the GMB have
been learning from these indie unions,[4] and also that the changing
composition of the working class in Britain and the proliferation of
precarious employment have forced unions to change in order to
stay relevant.[5] It is also worth noting that the GMB operates a federal
structure, in which each region has considerable autonomy.[6] My
fieldwork found this ethos of decentralization to also be consistently
evident within the Midlands region, as well as in the region's relation
to the national centre, with the Regional Secretary showing a high

level of trust in senior organizers, who in turn placed confidence in more junior organizers to decide how to undertake delegated areas of work. This may help to explain how the GMB was capable of such agility and innovation in its work at BHX4, and is highly significant given the difficulties that unions often experience in transforming their practices when they have very longstanding structures and cultures.[7]

A book recently published by the GMB entitled *Uprising: The GMB Union's Experience of Race and Class*[8] offers a highly reflexive and self-critical assessment of the union's past and present. That the union should put resources into such a text reflects a recognition, in the words of the book's authors, that the union needs 'to engage with the new and vibrant Global Majority communities that [are] transforming the nature of work'.[9] This is particularly important for the GMB, as Karen Atkinson puts it her contribution to *Uprising*, 'because of the unequal conditions governing labour we represent those on the lowest grades of pay, where Black people – and migrant workers – are disproportionately concentrated'.[10] Drawing on *Uprising* alongside the academic literature helps to keep this chapter grounded in the union's day-to-day struggles, and is consistent with the methodology of co-production that was applied to analyse the GMB's practices at BHX4.[11]

Nosakhere and Callow situate their book within a recent turn by the GMB towards directly addressing race, after a mixed history. They describe a report on race in the GMB, written by academic Elizabeth Henry in 2002 in response to the Macpherson Inquiry following the murder of Stephen Lawrence, which Henry describes in her Foreword to *Uprising* as having been 'quietly shelved, more than half forgotten'.[12] Henry's report was retrieved in 2022 as part of a process of deep reflection that was prompted by a crisis of sexism in the highest levels of the union and a resulting Taskforce for Positive Change. This Taskforce created space for a long process of organizing by Global Majority members to bear fruit. Discussions on race were reopened, leading to the appointment of the union's first National Race Organizer and the creation of a Race Achievement Scholarship Programme (GRASP) that aimed to develop the next generation of Global Majority leaders.[13] This is important to the BHX4 campaign, because as Mustchin identifies, internal union politics are extremely important in terms of how unions go about organizing migrant workers.[14]

These recent developments are part of a long history of anti-racist struggle within the union. Nosakhere and Callow emphasize the thread of internationalist anti-capitalism that Global Majority activists have frequently brought to the union, arguing that this is an important corrective to forms of trade unionism that they describe as characterized by a 'lack of purpose, drift, and abandonment of both ideology and ideals, in favour of simple wage bargaining, social compromise, and an unthinking Labourism – expecting outside forces and a political party to deliver gains, rather than identifying and delivering them for ourselves'.[15] The accounts of Global Majority members gathered within *Uprising* also speak of ongoing challenges within the union, with former Central Executive Council (CEC) member Robbie Scott arguing: 'As we look for the future leaders of our union, it is crucial to confront the stark reality of the under-representation of Black workers across our movement.'[16] This further highlights the importance of the union's achievements at BHX4, including the development of many outstanding Global Majority leaders.

The contradictions over race and migration within the GMB's history are exemplified by Nosakhere and Callow's chapter on the Grunwick dispute in 1976. They highlight the inspirational grassroots leadership of Jayaben Desai and other members of the APEX union, which would later merge with the GMB, yet also the failure of union leaders to adequately support the strike. This led to the hunger strike by Desai and other Grunwick leaders on the steps of the TUC, in protest at their betrayal, to which APEX responded by suspending the hunger strikers from membership. Nosakhere and Callow describe this as 'one of the darkest days for the GMB "family" of trade unions',[17] yet also note the award of a Gold Badge – the GMB's highest honour – to Desai at the GMB's annual congress in 2007, as part of a process of self-criticism and renewal.

Continuing this process, the GMB established an Equality through Inclusion strategy in 2008, which Nosakhere and Callow argue 'made clear that the fight for Equality was not just the responsibility of groups who had been discriminated against but of everyone'.[18] There were various attempts in this period to engage with migrants, including those from the Eastern European countries that had recently gained the right to work in the UK through European Union (EU) citizenship. For example, the GMB's Southern region engaged in a partnership with the Midwest European Communities Association (MECA) community organization in Somerset and created a dedicated migrant workers' branch in Southampton, accompanied by an English for Speakers of Other Languages (ESOL) programme.[19] Mustchin documents the same migrant workers' branch, finding that it had some success in identifying workplaces as potential targets for more focused organizing, developing 'informal shop stewards', improving migrant workers' confidence to represent themselves and recruiting at least one Polish woman worker as a paid organizer.[20] However, Mustchin reports that 'the migrant workers' branch in this form was short-lived, as the breadth and complexity of individual, often non-employment related issues dealt with were not matched with commensurate improvements in workplace organization and recruitment'.[21] The GMB's North West region also experimented with ESOL provision and some partnerships with migrant community organizations in this period. Although Mustchin describes this as 'patchy' and facing some opposition within the union, he reports that it succeeded in recruiting some migrant workers as workplace reps. *Uprising* cites other successes organizing Global Majority workers around the same time as including 'the Carillion workers in Croydon hospital, where we challenged a bad employer, campaigning around low pay, racial harassment, mistreatment and bullying, and successfully recruited from a wonderful pool of activists as a consequence'.[22] In the same period, Holgate describes the union's engagement with community organizing, arguing that this was driven in large part by a concern to engage with migrant and minority ethnic communities with which the union had little contact. Yet, the systematic approach that this sought to establish, which in 2008 Holgate says was intended to be 'formalised and systemised through GMB's national policy frameworks',[23] seems to have left little lasting impact. *Uprising* describes these advances being pushed back from 2012, arguing that this was caused by formalism and careerism.[24]

Alongside such targeted campaigns organizing with migrant workers, the GMB was also involved in a series of disputes during 2009–2010 regarding the engineering construction sector, in which issues of migration and divides along lines of nationality and language were central.[25] These strikes began on 28 January 2009, when workers at Lindsey Oil Refinery in north Lincolnshire were told that IREM, an Italian company that was due to take over a third of the contract on behalf of the French multinational Total, was refusing to employ British labour. Another subcontractor, Shaw's, had issued 90-day redundancy notices in mid-November, meaning that workers already facing redundancy in mid-February would not be allowed to apply for the IREM jobs. They were also told that the Italian and Portuguese workers whom IREM was planning to employ would be housed on floating barges for the duration of the job and would be bussed back to the barges for lunch. This was understandably interpreted by many workers as an attempt to keep them separate from British workers and trade unions. While media coverage of this dispute focused on the use of the slogan 'British Jobs for British Workers' by a minority of workers, who were quoting then Prime Minister Gordon Brown, this was never endorsed by the GMB or the grassroots strike committee, which instead put forward demands that included an end to the segregation of workers, the extension of the national agreement to all workers in Britain (migrant workers being exempt under the EU Posted Workers Directive) and union support for migrant workers.[26]

More recently, alongside its work at Amazon, the GMB has moved into parts of the 'gig economy' that have very high concentrations of migrant workers, including formal recognition agreements with app-based private hire and delivery operators Uber and Deliveroo. These agreements were signed after a protracted legal challenge by Uber drivers – some of whom were supported by the GMB – forced Uber to offer 'worker status' to its drivers, bringing with it a form of hourly minimum pay and holiday and sickness protections. The GMB has faced criticism from some who argue that these companies sought agreements with the GMB as a public relations exercise or to undermine the more militant organizing of 'indie' unions like the Independent Workers' Union of Great Britain (IWGB) and the App Drivers and Couriers Union (ADCU).[27] Yet, the GMB reports that it has won concessions from these companies since receiving recognition, including a minimum pay floor, expenses payments and delivery weight restrictions for Deliveroo riders,[28] and the ability to have representation in appeals against deactivations from the Uber app.[29]

Within the Midlands region, where Coventry is located, GMB officers described gaining valuable experience for the BHX4 campaign from having organized with another linguistically and ethnically diverse workforce at CNC Speedwell. In that campaign, organizers consulted with the entire membership at each stage of the negotiations, leading to the rejection of a 10 per cent pay offer that had been negotiated by organizers and the eventual winning of a 20 per cent increase. A senior organizer said that the lesson they took from this dispute was to never think that officers know better than the workers, and linked this dispute to a deep cultural shift within the region towards more ambitious action.[30] Yet GMB organizers made no reference to any of the union's other experiences with migrant workers described earlier in this chapter as informing their work at BHX4. This suggests that the GMB has considerable capacity for local innovation, but perhaps faces difficulties in terms of embedding and sharing the lessons of local campaigns to inform long-term development across the organization.

The GMB's organizing strategy at Amazon

The GMB's approach at BHX4 built on an 'organizing model' of trade unionism, which was widely promoted among British trade unions by the TUC Organising Academy in the early 2000s.[31] Gregor Gall describes organizing as involving an 'orientation to the self-activity of workers in the workplace and self-determination of agenda by the individual groups of workers concerned', in contrast to a 'service model' of trade unionism that is 'more akin to a business transaction for the delivery of a service by the union through its full-time officials'.[32] The GMB's National Organising Strategy and associated training for worker-leaders and organizers are built around five principles:

1. The workplace is the building block of the GMB.
2. Each workplace should be organized as if a ballot for action was due.
3. The employer has different interests than GMB members.
4. It is the process of industrial relations that builds the GMB, not the result.
5. People are strongest when they organize themselves.[33]

These principles express an underlying commitment to continuous workplace organizing, member empowerment and readiness for confrontation. This outlook corresponds to an approach to trade unionism advocated by Little, Sharp, Stevenson and Wilson, in which: 'Organised collectives of workers, built from the workplace up, are the point of the union, and all other structures – national executives, regional offices, local districts, negotiators and officers – are auxiliary, and should be geared towards building and strengthening these collectives.'[34]

Midlands GMB organizers expressed their central goal at BHX4 in the form of a 'commander's intent': 'An Active Unionised Workplace that achieves real benefits for our members inside Amazon.'[35] The GMB's National Organising Strategy identifies three conditions for the success of a campaign: *access* to the workplace; an *issue* that is widely and deeply felt among the workers; and *momentum* in the sense of workers moving together towards their goal. While the wildcat protests in August 2022 represented considerable momentum around a clear unifying issue of pay, access to the workplace was limited in multiple ways: GMB organizers did not have a recognition agreement; Amazon management were strongly opposed to any union presence; the activity of workers within the workplace was tightly controlled; and multiple cross-cutting divisions among the workforce meant that in most cases, even workers themselves had limited access to other workers. The easy option would have been to give up and for organizers to shift their attention to other workplaces where their tried-and-tested methods were already effective. But Midlands GMB organizers recognized the significance of Amazon for the future of work, and reasoned that if they could not find ways to organize effectively under the conditions that Amazon presented, then the future of the union and its members was bleak. This led to a determined process of innovation and the transformation of many of the union's usual practices, producing important lessons, especially for other contexts where access is limited.

In developing their approach at Amazon, some GMB organizers cited the influence of organizer and academic Jane McAlevey,[36] whose work they considered particularly relevant because of her experience in successfully organizing migrant workers in contexts where the union lacked access, and her detailed accounts of how these fights were won. It should be noted that McAlevey acknowledges that there is nothing fundamentally new in her approach, but rather that it captures lessons from trade unionism dating back to the 1930s, which are sometimes forgotten. Taking a lead from the repeated references to McAlevey by some GMB organizers, this book therefore draws on McAlevey's systematic approach to 'deep organizing', together with other relevant parts of the organizing literature, to develop a strengths-based analysis of the GMB's organizing strategy. This analysis works with the central premises and goals of organizing as cited by GMB organizers and elaborated by McAlevey, and uses these to identify the distinctive strengths of the GMB's organizing practices at BHX4, to reflect on how they could be further developed and to draw lessons with wider relevance.

To clarify the use of terminology, McAlevey generally refers to paid employees of a trade union as 'organizers', while GMB literature often refers to them as 'officers', and McAlevey describes union members who play a leading role but are not employed by the union as 'worker-leaders' or 'natural leaders', while the GMB normally refers to them as 'workplace organizers'. While I initially suggested using the GMB's terminology for consistency, senior organizers/officers involved in the BHX4 campaign proposed that McAlevey's terminology of organizers and worker-leaders captures the reality of this process more effectively, so those are the terms that are used in this book.

The GMB's approach at BHX4 placed a strong emphasis on democracy by involving workers in every decision and investing considerable time and resources in supporting the development of worker-leaders. McAlevey argues that trade union organizing is centrally important for democracy under capitalism.[37] The systematic attention to power and the wider politics of organizing is something that Holgate argues has generally been missing from British trade unionism, which she says has often assumed that recruiting more members represents an equivalent increase in power.[38] GMB organizers at BHX4 showed no such assumption and instead viewed the strength of the union at BHX4 as directly dependent on the level of engagement and self-leadership among the members.

Consistent with this emphasis on democracy, McAlevey urges union organizers to trust workers, to take their perspectives seriously and to systematically build their power within the organizing process.[39] This attitude was clearly evident in the GMB approach at BHX4. It is an integral part of what McAlevey describes as 'organizing' or sometimes 'deep organizing' – reaching out to those workers who may initially be hostile or indifferent to the union, to understand their concerns and grievances, and to persuade them that working as part of the union is the best route to achieving and protecting the things that matter to them.[40] Allinson describes the potential for such 'structure-based organizing': 'to involve a majority of a target group, which is inherently more powerful than a [self-selecting] scattered minority ... you are winning over and organising new people ... built around existing relationships between workers, making stronger bonds of solidarity'.[41] This requires mapping the workforce, and identifying and recruiting worker-leaders who have genuine influence with their colleagues, often being some of the most skilled and hardworking workers, and not necessarily among those initially inclined to join a union. This was systematically applied at BHX4, as discussed in Chapter 3. McAlevey counterpoises this to approaches that only mobilize those who are already in agreement.

Informed by the work of Brazilian educator Paulo Freire and her experience working at the Highlander Centre in Tennessee, McAlevey views organizing as fundamentally a form of education not through didactic lectures, but by creating situations that allow workers to learn things for themselves that can increase their power.[42] One element of this approach is supporting workers to undertake a 'power-structure analysis'.[43] The first part of this analysis involves an assessment of the 'whole worker', moving beyond the workplace to all the social networks that workers belong to, from family and friends to religious, sporting and cultural communities, who might become workers' allies in struggles with their employer. The second part of a power-structure analysis considers the social, economic and political context for the employer in order to identify actors outside the company who have power and influence over its practices. These ideas were embodied in many aspects of the GMB's approach at BHX4, including the education of worker-leaders (Chapter 5), the responses to workers' needs (Chapter 6) and the engagement with other institutional actors that had power to influence the company (Chapter 7).

Alongside the systematic building, and analysis, of power, McAlevey advocates 'starting quietly' and undertaking regular 'structure tests' to build trust and confidence among workers, and give organizers and worker-leaders a realistic assessment of the numbers and willingness of workers to take a particular form of action at a given point.[44] Examples of structure tests might include petitions, protests, consultative ballots or time-limited strikes. The underlying intention is that before the union seeks any definitive confrontation, such as a recognition ballot or an all-out strike, they will already be confident that they command a 'supermajority' of support among the workers and that they therefore have the committed numbers they need to win. This aims to reduce the risk of demoralizing defeats and is borne out by many successful examples that McAlevey provides, mostly in the intensely anti-union climate of the US. The complexities involved in applying this idea at BHX4 are discussed in Chapters 3 and 4, including the effective use of minority strikes to build the membership and the state regulations and employer tactics that would likely have rendered any prior structure test meaningless by the time a recognition ballot took place.

The literature outlined in this chapter was used alongside a deep immersion in the GMB's practice at BHX4 to structure the analysis of major challenges the GMB faced and the ways in which the union responded, which is presented in the following chapters.

Notes

[1] Callow, J. (2012) *GMB@Work: The Story behind the Union*, London: GMB.

[2] Bailey, D.J. (2024) 'Worker-led dissent in the age of austerity: comparing the conditions of success', *Work, Employment and Society*, 38(4): 1041–1061; McBride, J., Stirling, J. and Winter, S. (2013) ' "Because we were living it": the hidden work of a strike', *Work, Employment and Society*, 27(2): 244–253.

[3] Però, D. (2020) 'Indie unions, organising and labour renewal: learning from precarious migrant workers', *Work, Employment and Society*, 34(5): 900–918; Holgate, J. (2021) *Arise: Power, Strategy and Union Resurgence*, London: Pluto Press.

[4] Smith, H. (2022) 'The "indie unions" and the UK labour movement: towards a community of practice', *Economic and Industrial Democracy*, 43(3): 1369–1390.

[5] Alberti, G., Holgate, J. and Tapia, M. (2013) 'Organising migrants as workers or as migrant workers? Intersectionality, trade unions and precarious work', *International Journal of Human Resource Management*, 24(22): 4132–4148; Johnson, M. and Herman, E. (2024) 'Out with the old, in with the new? Institutional experimentation and decent

work in the UK', *Economic and Industrial Democracy*, DOI:10.1177/ 0143831X231220528.

6   Mustchin, S. (2012) 'Unions, learning, migrant workers and union revitalization in Britain', *Work, Employment and Society*, 26(6): 951–967.

7   Holgate, J. (2021) 'Trade unions in the community: building broad spaces of solidarity', *Economic and Industrial Democracy*, 42(2): 226–247.

8   Nosakhere, T. and Callow, J. (2024) *Uprising: The GMB Union's Experience of Race and Class*, London: GMB.

9   Nosakhere and Callow (n 8), p 19.

10 Nosakhere and Callow (n 8), p 175.

11 See Appendix 2 for details.

12 Nosakhere and Callow (n 8), p 15.

13 Nosakhere and Callow (n 8), pp 145–147.

14 Mustchin (n 6).

15 Nosakhere and Callow (n 8), p 178.

16 Nosakhere and Callow (n 8), p 161.

17 Nosakhere and Callow (n 8), p 99.

18 Nosakhere and Callow (n 8), p 128.

19 Jiang, J. and Korczynski, M. (2024) 'The role of community organisations in the collective mobilisation of migrant workers: the importance of a "community"-oriented perspective', *Work, Employment and Society*, 38(2): 339–357; Alberti, Holgate and Tapia (n 5).

20 Mustchin (n 6).

21 Mustchin (n 6), p 959.

22 Jandu, in Nosakhere and Callow (n 8), p 129.

23 Holgate, J. (2013) 'Community organising in the UK: A "new" approach for trade unions?', *Economic and Industrial Democracy*, 36(3): 431–455, at 446.

24 Jandu, in Nosakhere and Callow (n 8), p 129.

25 Gall, G. (2009) 'The engineering construction strikes in Britain, 2009', *Capital and Class*, 36(3): 411–431.

26 Vickers, T. (2019) *Borders, Migration and Class: Producing Immigrants and Workers*, Bristol: Bristol University Press, pp 50–53.

27 Bernal, N. (2021) 'Uber's union deal in the UK doesn't mean its battles are over', *Wired UK*, [online] 27 May, Available from: https://www. wired.com/story/uber-union-deal-uk/ [Accessed 8 November 2024]; Butler, S. (2022) 'Deliveroo accused of "cynical PR move" with union deal for couriers', *The Guardian*, [online] 12 May, Available from: https://www.theguardian.com/business/2022/may/12/delive roo-union-deal-couriers-minimum-wage-gmb-iwgb [Accessed 8 November 2024].

[28] GMB (2024a) 'Deliveroo noticeboard', [online], Available from: https://www.gmb.org.uk/private-sector/logistics/deliveroo-hub [Accessed 11 November 2024].

[29] GMB (2021) 'The union for Uber drivers', [online], Available from: https://www.gmb.org.uk/assets/media/downloads/1222/NEW-UBER-A5-LEAFLET%20-%20UPDATED%2019-11-21.pdf [Accessed 11 November 2024).

[30] Fieldnotes 16 January 2024, 17 September 2024.

[31] Simms, M., Holgate, J. and Heery, E. (2013) *Union Voices: Tactics and Tensions in UK Organizing*, Ithaca, NY: Cornell University Press.

[32] Gall, G. (2005) 'Organizing non-union workers as trade unionists in the "new economy" in Britain', *Economic and Industrial Democracy*, 26(1): 41–63, at 42.

[33] GMB (2024) 'Make work better: GMB workplace representatives and shop stewards induction course, part 1 (Autumn 2024–Summer 2025 ed.)', p 26.

[34] Little, G., Sharp, E., Stevenson, H. and Wilson, D. (2023) *Lessons in Organising: What Trade Unionists Can Learn from the War on Teachers*, London: Pluto Press, p 146.

[35] Fieldnotes 17 September 2024.

[36] McAlevey, J.F. (2012) *Raising Expectations (and Raising Hell): My Decade Fighting for the Labor Movement*, London: Verso; McAlevey, J.F. (2016) *No Shortcuts: Organizing for Power*, Oxford: Oxford University Press; McAlevey, J.F. (2021) 'Jane McAlevey', podcast interviews, in P. Jay (ed.), Available from: theAnalysis.news; McAlevey, J.F. (2023) *Rules to Win By: Power and Participation in Union Negotiations*, Oxford: Oxford University Press.

[37] McAlevey (2023) (n 36), pp 7–11.

[38] Holgate (n 3), p 130.

[39] McAlevey (2021) (n 36), pt 2/8.

[40] McAlevey (2016) (n 36), pp 9–13; McAlevey (2021) (n 36), pt 5/8.

[41] Allinson, I. (2022) *Workers Can Win: A Guide to Organising at Work*, London: Pluto Press, p 28.

[42] McAlevey (2012) (n 36), pp 17–18, 133–135.

[43] McAlevey (2016) (n 36), pp 2–9; McAlevey (2021) (n 36), pt 7/8; McAlevey (2023) (n 36), pp 35–40.

[44] McAlevey (2023) (n 36), pp 43–45.

ESSAY 2

Managing an Organizing Team in the Amazon Campaign

Amanda Gearing, GMB Senior Organizer

The Midlands Organizing Team that I manage gives us the flexibility to direct resources quickly to respond to opportunities and bolster particular campaigns. I have been a GMB organizer since 2007 and a Senior Organizer since 2012. In 2018, I did a management apprenticeship that transformed my management practice and changed my life. We looked at autonomy and mastery. How we all need ownership over our work and to feel that we are achieving. I started to ask myself why I was checking diaries to make sure they were full when I should have been focusing on the results. Why did I think I had all the answers when I had six people in the team out, on the ground, in workplaces day in day out? I realized that my team meetings were just me talking and people trying to guess what I wanted them to say, instead of being creative thinkers or problem solvers, instead of challenging the norm and sharing their ideas.

When it came to team meetings, we scrapped agendas. If I needed to communicate any procedural information, I would send an email. Our time together is precious, it should be spent developing our campaigns and ideas, reviewing campaigns that are already in motion, understanding our direction of travel, creating our 'commander's intent' and, most importantly, getting to know one another, strengthening our bonds.

We regularly perform an Action Learning Set (ALS), which is designed to identify goals and allow a creative process for the actions/ideas to get you there. The particular approach we use for this is STOPP:

- *Situation* = What do we know right now?
- *Target* = What do we want to achieve?
- *Opportunities* = This is the magic bit! The whole team gets to throw in their ideas, even if they are a bit off the wall. It's fun and it's good for the team, but it also makes space for you to trust that ideas can't be criticized at this stage. It really works – the ideas flow and through the fun, it brings energy and gets us out of the box and on a road to success.
- *Pitfalls and Payoffs* = This is the part where we evaluate the ideas. You go through each one individually, assess whether it is going to help us reach the target we have set and either get rid of the ones that don't fit or keep the ones that further us towards our goal.

Once this process is over, you have the bones of the plan; you just need to put it into your timeline and allocate areas for ownership.

This process helps the team to buy in, to get motivated and excited; you start to see if the lead/project has merit, how long it will take and what order the tasks need to be put in. It also enables me to see the resource we will need at each stage.

With Amazon, we ran ALSs on a regular basis. We ran them with both teams that worked on the project, which included support staff and workplace leaders. We had sessions where we would review progress; sometimes our initial targets would drift and the results would show that, so we would reset the situation. Getting the buy-in from everyone wasn't always easy, there were long hours, some tasks like phone banking were unpopular, but the reviews enabled us to work through some of the gripes. There was always a compromise or a reminder of what we needed to do to meet our goals that could bring us back on track. Sometimes we all need a moan, and space was needed for that as well, as long as all problems were met with solutions, we kept moving forward. Sometimes I also invited senior management to join us; it helps to have those that hold the ultimate say in the room and to keep them invested in what we're doing. By far the most successful reviews were those that included the workplace leaders, as the perspective they brought often resulted in a change of direction.

Going from telling to coaching and mentoring has been a game changer. I don't have all the answers, but I don't need to; I often find the team do, I just have to squeeze it out. You might ask how do you know what your team's strengths and weaknesses are, I could talk about DISC profiling (a form of personality assessment) and doing a SWOT (strengths, weaknesses, opportunities and threats) analysis, all may be useful, but my advice would be to leave your office and go out into the field with them. During the Amazon campaign, I attended every picket line. I was part of developing the leaders, I worked on the WhatsApp groups, answering questions, building relationships with contacts, etc. I observed the team, looked at where they placed themselves, what they volunteered for, how they mixed with members, how they handled difficult situations, who was joining people up and much more. This gave me much more insight.

As part of any plan, there has to be time for reviews and structure tests, this helps to keep the resources tight and get the maximum outcomes. In the Amazon campaign, we used many forms of structure test, from registering workers for strikes, to providing leaders with QR codes to distribute surveys to members (which enabled us to track how much engagement leaders were having), to assigning tasks around translations.

In summary, the Amazon campaign required me to deploy resources fast initially. I had to assess the merits of the campaign by listening and working the ideas through a process, identifying what success looked like and then directing the resources at the different stages. I also had to identify the correct people in the team to share leadership of the campaign.

If I was to say what makes a good organizer, then it would have to be the ability to actively listen to members and workplace leaders. To problem solve and have the ability to know when to take a risk. To also be able to bring their own drive and determination. To create trust among the individuals and me, and between the team as a whole. To allow the risks that can come with high rewards, the team have to know you back them and will be there to help them if it doesn't work. The team also have permission to tell me if they think I'm wrong and they often do.

To have the kind of creatives you need in an organizing team, you have to create a space for that; the change in style of the team meetings and one-to-ones helped with that. My teams' diaries are full to bursting but every meeting, visit, event, planning session now has purpose – the emphasis being on reaching your picture of success instead of how many canteens you visited that week. If you can bear to follow this your team will flourish. And review, review, review!

I believe that the success of this campaign came from the unrelenting dedication and motivation of the team, and I feel proud that the changes that I made set us on the rollercoaster of achievement.

3

Reaching
the Whole Workforce

Fundamentally, the organizing model of trade unionism relies on workers' collective power and, all other things being equal, it is therefore more effective when a larger proportion of workers are actively involved.[1] This is expressed in the GMB organizing principle that 'The workplace is the building block of the GMB',[2] which implies that the strength of the union relies on organization across each workplace. In the current UK context, a company is forced to formally recognize any union that can demonstrate that more than 50 per cent of workers in a defined 'bargaining unit' (for example, all workers in the same role in a given warehouse) support the union. This creates a legislative incentive to secure what McAlevey calls a 'supermajority', meaning a clear majority of workers who are prepared to act together. This chapter discusses the challenges that the GMB faced reaching the whole workforce at BHX4 and how it responded.

Challenges in reaching the whole workforce

This section explores how the spatial and temporal structure of the warehouse created difficulties for organizers to reach the workforce, and even for workers to speak to each other, followed by challenges associated with the demographic composition of the workforce, the social situation of workers outside the warehouse and the turnover of workers.

BHX4 is a highly controlled work environment, union organizers are not allowed access outside of direct invitations to represent members in formal meetings, and workers describe their roles as strictly monitored and often isolating. The strict labour discipline within the warehouse is illustrated by the following description of how managers responded to workers showing signs of tiredness:

> You're ten hours on your feet and if you get caught sat down, you're in trouble … one lad that used to work opposite me was sat down and a manager … said: 'Are you comfortable?' And he was like: 'Yeah.' [The manager] said: 'Why are you sitting down?' He said: 'I'm tired.' [The manager] said: 'OK … I want you to empty everybody's bin, give your legs some exercise.' And he had to go around the whole of upstairs, and we're talking probably … close to 300 stations … which was just demeaning … another lad that I used to work with … yawned and the manager said: 'Are you tired?' And he was like: 'Yeah, a bit.' He [the manager] said: 'Go and get yourself a coffee.' He's like: 'Really?' He says: 'Yeah, go and get yourself a coffee.' And then they did [disciplined] him for having an extra break. (European worker-leader GA-02)

Adding to the difficulty that such strict control created for conversation between workers, worker-leaders described needing to spend ten minutes of their 30-minute lunch break queuing for food, in addition to the time taken to walk to and from the canteen, leaving little time for purposeful conversations.[3] There were also reports of time spent talking to colleagues being classified as 'idle time' and added together as grounds for 'ADAPTs', standing for Associate Development and Performance Tracker, a notice on a worker's record that can lead to a formal disciplinary process.[4] Worker-leaders reported that the threshold for the number of ADAPTs needed to trigger a disciplinary process was reduced in 2024 from three in six weeks to two in six weeks, and there were numerous reports of workers not being told when they had been issued an ADAPT, only finding out once they had accrued enough to hit the threshold for disciplinary action.[5] Worker-leaders described managers as having a considerable amount of discretion over how they added together brief pauses to justify

ADAPTs for accumulated 'idle time', making it easy for managers to practise favouritism:

> [T]he timing between the single scan, they are including in their idle time … We are not robot[s] … We [are] scanning the item, [it] take[s] time, like 30 seconds or 20 seconds. So, they [are] including all the seconds, 20 seconds, one minute … and then, and at the end of the shift, they said: 'Oh, you … have idle time [totalling] three hours or four hours.' They are behaving like this, even though sometimes line is dry, there is no work on the line … You go to toilet, you go to for water … everything is included … they are hiding behind the system. So, this is all the pressure. (Global Majority worker-leader GA-15)

The calculation of time spent on productive mobility for Amazon versus rest for the worker expresses a stark contradiction, calling to mind the GMB organizing principle that: 'The employer has different interests than GMB members.'[6] This suggests an approach that has the appearance of formal equality because activity is monitored through a digital system, but this is combined with subjective judgements by managers about how to apply these measurements. These disciplinary mechanisms can therefore easily be targeted at workers who are trying to unionize with colleagues.

Further challenges arose from the spatial and temporal arrangements of the workplace. The BHX4 warehouse was massive, designed to accommodate 1,650 workers and employing 3,012 by July 2024. Workers were divided across multiple floors, departments and lines, and were further divided between day and night shifts patterns referred to as 'front-end' (Sunday–Wednesday), 'back-end' (Wednesday–Saturday), 'donut' (Monday, Tuesday, Thursday and Friday), 'double donut' (Monday, Tuesday, Friday and Saturday), and full-time, part-time and 'flexi' contracts. These cross-cutting spatial and temporal divisions combined with the strict labour discipline outlined in this chapter to mean that any one worker-leader usually had direct access to only a limited number of their colleagues within the workplace.

The BHX4 workforce was further divided by nationality and language – one experienced worker-leader told me that he had counted 26 different languages being spoken within BHX4, and a Freedom of Information request I submitted to the UK Home Office revealed that during the year to 30 September 2023, Amazon UK sponsored visas for workers from 86 countries. The following quotation illustrates the challenges this created for organizing:

> Probably the main challenge was ... the language barrier... because it was so hard and people don't understand [what is a] Union ... I think it was Romanian that when we did the translation, I think it was on Google, 'union' in Romanian is like a syndicate, organized crime! (European worker-leader GA-02)

Another worker-leader commented regarding workers' mixed understanding of unions that many of them 'come from countries where striking is almost like a forbidden thing' (European worker-leader GA-04). Another worker-leader, themselves a migrant, reported finding 'so many colleagues who cannot understand ... English' (European migrant worker-leader GA-21). Some worker-leaders understood this as integral to Amazon's strategy, with one Global Majority worker-leader telling a meeting with colleagues, 'this company was designed to make money from immigrants, because we are not united'.[7]

Reaching workers outside the workplace was also challenging because many lived far from the warehouse and were spread out, with some travelling in from other cities such as Birmingham and Leicester, and often working long hours that left little time for contact outside work. The standard full-time working week at BHX4 was 40 hours, but many workers reported feeling under financial pressure to take overtime, often working up to 60 hours per week at Amazon and/or taking additional work, as evidenced by the many workers seen arriving for their shift driving an Uber. Worker-leaders and organizers discussed the challenges this created getting workers to meetings, as illustrated by the following quotation:

> [W]e have been calling for maybe an online meeting, an all-hands meeting of how we can plan. I don't see such a number of us coming on, even online ... The reality

remains that due to the work schedule … whether it's at night or in the day, it's affecting our organizing system. Because if you're not working in the day, you're working at night. And no matter what time you're working, you don't have the time. (Global Majority worker-leader GA-05)

Thus, while workers inside the warehouse were divided in terms of time and space and had their mobility highly controlled, outside the warehouse they were scattered in space with little free time.

Lastly, there was a rapid turnover of the workforce, previously found to be as high as 150 per cent per year.[8] At least 1,500 new Associates were recruited to BHX4 in the year from May 2023 and according to an Amazon statement reported by the *Financial Times* on 12 July 2024, up to 49 per cent of its UK staff at that time were temporary. A worker-leader described the difficulties this created maintaining relationships with colleagues:

People just disappear from work. You know, one day you will see them there, and then all of a sudden you just … don't see them again. And so … I start asking … I said: 'I haven't seen him for a while, I thought … they moved to another FC [fulfilment centre].' And then I realized, somebody told me … he was fired. (Global Majority worker-leader GA-01)

Such rapid fluctuations meant that the task of reaching the whole workforce was never complete, and required sustained and intensive work.

Together, these challenges amounted to a highly fragmented context in which to organize, with workers scattered, contained and isolated from one another and from union organizers by multiple intersecting divides. To collectivize across these boundaries required a combination of using Amazon's own structures to reach across divides within the warehouse and find pockets of time and space in which to autonomously move, contesting with Amazon's control where possible, and also creating entirely new spaces outside of Amazon's control, particularly through the creative use of what I call 'strike time'.

The GMB's response to reach the whole workforce

This section explores how the GMB reached the workforce at BHX4. This began with slow and steady preparatory work over years of casework and campaigning, and then a sudden acceleration of organizing to capitalize on the spontaneous moment of unity that was provoked by a lower-than-expected pay increase in August 2022. I trace the meeting point that resulted from a mobilization of organizers towards the warehouse in combination with the self-organized movement of workers out into the relative autonomy of the streets. The success of this meeting between the formal structures of the union and the spontaneous initiative of the workers, in which both were willing to be transformed, then led to the sustained and legally protected space created by official strikes. Through these strikes, workers built confidence that fed back into the warehouse to support challenges to Amazon's regime of control.

While the organizing drive at BHX4 took off in August 2022, it was only possible because of longer-term work by the GMB. This established relationships with a small number of initial members who brought the organizers in to quickly build on the wildcat walkouts. This work began at Amazon's Rugeley BHX1 site in 2012, where organizers began recruiting workers at the gate and won some small-scale victories through individual representations and getting a new toilet block built. They did not succeed at this stage in connecting with organic leaders among the workers, but learned important lessons, as an organizer explained:

> So, we just started to hang around on the gate really and talk ... Although our membership did increase during that period, but our focus was on, mobilizing really, higher overarching type campaigns about ambulances, about health and safety, that kind of thing. We got to know a couple of people that ... did the training and became reps. But I think, looking back, they weren't the right people to have been leaders within there. (European organizer GA-09)

A claim for formal recognition at BHX1 was withdrawn after it became clear that the workforce was larger than the union had thought, and so the percentage who were GMB members was too low to secure a ballot. This experience provided valuable lessons about Amazon's employment practices and a small initial base of members, some of whom were internally transferred to BHX4 when it opened in 2017. Organizers described how their organizing practice changed over this period, informed by their experience at BHX1 and in other campaigns:

> I think as an organizing team … we've [grown] a lot in understanding what we need to do and what we're looking for in people. And we've learned lessons over … years … and how we organize now is very different to how we organized in Rugeley, completely flipped on its head. (European organizer GA-08)

The GMB's work at Amazon continued during the worst parts of the COVID-19 pandemic, including casework with individual members and petitions protesting over what were felt by the union to be inadequate Personal Protective Equipment (PPE) for workers and management-imposed practices that made it impossible for workers to socially distance. This work meant that when the wildcat protests occurred in 2022, the GMB was already known to some of the leaders, who phoned GMB organizers and enabled them to respond immediately and begin signing up more members, as an organizer explained:

> [T]he organizers that were looking after that site [BHX4] … did a lot of work representing and building up our credibility and rapport … which then grew our membership slightly… [An organizer] did a lot of work around … the health and safety aspect with COVID … So, all of that time there was a presence, there was a connection. There [was] a relationship being built … and then when it all kicked off [in 2022] … those workers knew that they could reach out to us and we'd be able to support them. (European organizer GA-08)

The August 2022 protests were sparked by the announcement of a 50 pence per hour wage increase. This occurred at a time when inflation was 12.3 per cent, which was felt particularly acutely in terms of food prices.[9] Prior to this, worker-leaders and organizers reported real terms pay having fallen 22.6 per cent since 2018, notwithstanding a temporary increase and a one-off bonus during the worst part of the pandemic, and said that managers had talked about the August pay rise in a way that raised expectations.[10] Similar responses were evident among Amazon workers elsewhere – for example, in the same year, workers at Winsen in Germany striked across multiple shifts, sparked by the announcement of a 3 per cent pay rise when inflation was 10 per cent.[11]

At BHX4, multiple worker-leaders described how their objection to the 50 pence pay rise was rooted in an awareness of Amazon's huge wealth and profits: 'Amazon went: "Great news, here's the 50p pay rise." We were like, "50p, what's 50p? We've just gone through all this stuff with COVID … Now, here's your great pay rise of 50p where you've just gone and made hundreds of millions of pounds in profits"' (European worker-leader GA-04).

Some worker-leaders contrasted this directly with rising costs of necessities:

> [E]lectricity and gas prices [had] gone up, even the rent were going up and everything is going up. So, we [were] expecting some good pay rise and … they didn't give us a good pay rise … And we made Amazon so much … profit. (Global Majority worker-leader GA-32)

This created a deeply felt resistance to worsening real pay, exacerbated by the gap between expectations and the actual pay rise, and catalysed into an intense sense of injustice by workers' understanding of the widening gap between their pay and Amazon's profits. This highlights the importance of political understanding, education and values, and consequent discursive framing in motivating workers to take action.[12]

These protests were further fuelled by ongoing concerns over health and safety, with examples described by worker-leaders at BHX4 including the unsafe management of a cardboard compactor, a lack of effective cooling in containers during hot weather, a lack of breaks to get water, and enforcement of work rates that were often felt to be both inflexible to individuals' needs and capacities and liable to subjective favouritism by managers.[13] Protests took place at multiple sites around the UK, starting in Tilbury, with workers hearing about each other's actions through TikTok and Telegram.[14] These protests were not purely spontaneous, but developed out of discussions between workers, who at BHX4 agreed to a sit-down protest in the cafeteria beginning during a break and continuing with a refusal to return to work. This represented an effective adaption to the spatial and temporal fragmentation of the workforce, by beginning action during a break time when workers from multiple departments would be in the same place at the same time.

The BHX4 General Manager addressed the protest in a way that multiple worker-leaders described as disrespectful, and invited a delegation to go upstairs to present demands. Worker-leaders who were present described this from their varying perspectives, for example:

> During our first sit-down strike, [the General Manager] was very rude to us … He treated us like dirt … He just [said], if you need [to] you write your … questions, and then ten questions, and I will answer them. So, I answered him right away: 'We don't need ten questions. We only need one question. When are you going to … increase our pay? That's the only question here. Nothing more.' And … he just turned his back and left. (Global Majority worker-leader GA-01)

Consistent with advice from GMB organizers, with whom some of the workers were in touch by phone, the workers refused the invitation to send a delegation upstairs and insisted that any negotiation should involve all of them, as another worker-leader described:

> [The General Manager] wanted to make a list of five people that could come upstairs and [saying]: 'We'll discuss your grievances in a proper manner.' … 'As soon as we go on them steps', I said, 'I could send my best friend up, and he could negotiate all he wants to, but if he comes back down with an undesirable number or being told that's it [no further pay rise], we're going to fall out then' … 'To split us', I said, 'don't do it. As

soon as we put a foot on them steps, we lose.' (European worker-leader GA-02)

This embodies McAlevey's principle of 'big and open negotiations'.[15] A GMB organizer argued that this marked a key difference from the Rugely site at that time, where workers accepted such an offer and thereby lost momentum and mass engagement:

> The leaders inside Rugeley that were leading those wildcat sit-ins didn't listen to us when I told them not to go into those meetings with management ... And they believed what the management was saying to them. And the management was like 'Yeah, we'll get back to you in a week', with this and that. And the momentum just died and [was] killed straight away. But with Coventry, because they stood there and they stood firm, that momentum continued. (European organizer GA-08)

When the protesting workers at BHX4 refused to send a delegation to negotiate, they were signed off work by management in a clear attempt to use the material pressure of wages to force them to return to work. This led workers to realize that they needed to find a time and space to organize beyond Amazon's control, and made plans to meet the following day.

As the protests at BHX4 continued into a second day and moved out of the controlled space of the workplace so that workers could talk to each other more freely in the autonomous space of the streets, union officers were quick to respond and sent out organizers to speak to workers and offer support. Worker-leaders described how:

> On the Friday, we then went into the city. We met at the Amazon car park. We stood around shouting 'No work today' ... The security came out and said: 'You have to leave the car park.' So, we went into town. At that point, I think basically this is where ... I think a few of them [workers] who had been members of the GMB before messaged them and said: 'Look guys, if you want in, this is the time to get into Amazon.' They [GMB organizers] all turned up in the city centre, gave us the leaflets, gave

us the documents, and said: 'Look, sign [up].' Then they
started running through the car park every night, almost
like routine, for three months, getting us to try and sign
members up. (European worker-leader GA-04)

An organizer described how they approached this self-organized
action, taking time to identify organic leaders:

That was an opportunity where I just needed to take a
couple of moments, and I just stood back and I looked
and I watched who everybody was going to and I went
to them first and had a conversation with them and
got their details. And I just grabbed a book and started
writing numbers down and then everybody that was
there will write their mobile number down. And I just
created a WhatsApp group and … in the end we had over
a thousand people across two WhatsApp groups within
a day. (European organizer GA-08)

Building directly on this worker-led action, the ethos of using strikes
as a protected form of protest over substantive issues − with the
demand for £15 per hour being central − became a central strategy
to reach more workers.

Minority strikes at BHX4 provided a means of organizing and
of leverage against the company, with formal recognition seen as a
potential consequence of the fight with the employer rather than
the central aim. This echoes strikes against Amazon in Germany
that began in 2013, which were pushed by workers who prioritized
issues of shop-floor control and saw strikes, even by a minority, as an
important part of an escalation strategy.[16] While Vgontzas argues that
these strikes later reached a point of 'stasis', Boewe and Schulten give
a more positive assessment, pointing to the persistence of strike action
amounting to more than 300 cumulative days by 2020, union density
between 30 and 50 per cent of permanent workers, and an estimated
14–17 per cent decrease in throughput of Amazon orders during
strike weeks.[17] This use of minority strikes might be interpreted as
contradicting McAlevey's advice to only strike with a supermajority,
but this would be neglecting her more fundamental argument to trust
the workers. Given the determination to protest by workers at BHX4

and the importance of strikes as a way of creating democratic space free from Amazon's control, the GMB's use of minority strikes was demonstrably an effective way to build the kind of worker power and voice that lies at the heart of McAlevey's approach.

GMB organizers explained that this approach of building the union through strikes from a small initial membership differed from their usual practice, where they would not consider balloting for industrial action before they had official recognition:

> So ... we found ourselves just evolving a strategy, which is start the fight first and go for recognition later. So, you're fighting on the substantive material things that matter to workers ... The union's just the vehicle through which you assert agency over your own life ... it's a very old idea, but it's been forgotten and lost and all we've done is apply it ... something that was reflecting back what people were saying to us, which was [saying to workers], 'The union provides you with a vehicle through which you can protest safely' ... and that came straight from the threats to people towards the end of the unofficial action in early August [2022] because ... management said: 'If you don't go back to work, we'll sign you off and you'll lose pay' ... people realized that 'Oh, we're not allowed to do this, what protection do we have?' ... And that's one of the reasons why people were saying: 'Look, we need a union here so we can be protected.' (European organizer GA-06)

Another organizer emphasised how these minority strikes were driven by the members:

> And that's when we started the consultative ballot for industrial action, because they had said to us what they wanted to do was to protest and not be sacked. And that's industrial action, it's the only way we know how to do that. And ... I think at the time we'd worked up to about 240 members ... and the consultative ballot, we had 300 people vote in it. So, they must have been passing the link around even though it was only sent

to members and I think it was 99 per cent voted in favour of strike action. So, it was a good mandate and some of the information we got from that ... we used to contact people that [weren't] members, [we] said, 'You voted in the consultative ballot, you're keen' ... normally ... you'll wait till you've got ... a lot of the membership before you start to take strike action and you would normally be recognized so you'd have access [to the workplace] ... Whereas we decided to use the dispute to drive the membership ... Now, I've been to a lot of picket lines and I've only ever seen like a handful of people join on a picket line ... and so I was a bit dubious. It was a risk ... But we went with what the members wanted. And I think that's the key thing that we probably haven't done so much in the past. We just kept listening ... I think it's changed the way that I look at organizing, I never look at a site as 'Oh, we're only 10 per cent so we'll have to wait until we're at 60 per cent' ... I say: 'What's the issue and how widely is it felt?'... 'What do the members think?' ... And: 'Are they willing to take action?' (European organizer GA-09)

This differed from many other British trade unions, with Gall describing 'a common perspective among trade unions which accords formal union recognition prime importance' and a consequent focus on 'the numbers game', resulting in a 'marked tendency to encourage membership passivity', 'to the detriment of the more qualitative aspects of degree of attachment and workplace organisation'.[18] Holgate's more recent assessment of British trade unions suggests that this continues to be the case.[19] While GMB organizers emphasized that this represented an important shift in their practice and organizational culture,[20] it could be seen as a logical development, to a higher level, of the GMB organizing principle that 'It is the process of industrial relations that builds the GMB not the result'.[21]

The first official strike at BHX4, following a successful ballot of members, began at a minute past midnight on 25 January 2023. Starting the strike at this time was not an intentional tactic, and it required workers to walk out in the middle of a shift, past lines of managers. Only a small number did so, but this set a tone of defiance on which the union would build over the coming months. A total of 37 days of strike action followed between January 2023 and June 2024, with many new members signing up on the picket line, in the weeks following a strike or in preparation for an impending strike.[22]

These strikes represented a release from Amazon's regimented mobility within the disciplined space-time of a warehouse shift, and an opportunity to freely associate with their workmates. Illustrating this, my fieldnotes recorded:

> Morning pickets were joyful, more and more workers taking to the centre of the road to speak to traffic [other Associates driving into work] until they reached all the way to the corner in an unbroken line. Estimate around 500 people in total … Evening picket was smaller but still significant (100–200 people).[23]

This atmosphere was summed up by a slide in a GMB presentation about the Amazon campaign, which stated: 'The picket line is a festival of the oppressed.'[24] The sense of temporary liberation brought about by strikes was further encouraged by timing strikes to coincide with religious festivals such as Eid and Orthodox Easter, which were important to large numbers of workers.

As the number of workers joining pickets built into the hundreds, these mass assemblies gave workers confidence to join the union with less fear that they would be singled out for victimization. A worker-leader described how this evolved:

> [On the first official strike at] exact[ly] 12 o'clock, the management … they are looking [at] us, we are just left our work and go there and very first night we have only 55 people … And then people start joining the union … every month when the strike … date is coming, how people come to us straight away … people know [we] are the pioneer people who are already in the joint union. They ask us: 'Oh, bro, I want to join union.' … And within … five minutes, even inside, we take [them] to the canteen … and we finished their membership. And slowly, we see that river is coming, drop, make a river and every month, 50, 150 people are including in the

union. And so far, we are around 1,200, almost 1,300 people. (Global Majority worker-leader GA-15)

GMB organizers and worker-leaders learned through a process of trial and error how to run a picket involving as many as 800 people and built this into an act of collective autonomous mobility, marching up the main road leading to the warehouse and organizing other members to flag down workers' cars and persuade them to join the strike. Some of the more experienced worker-leaders showed great skill in using anonymized case studies of workers' problems, and how the union had helped them, to recruit on the picket line.[25] A worker-leader described the inspiration of this experience and the role it played in his increasingly committed involvement in the union:

> [W]hen the amount of people I see, like night [shift] people and then day [shift] people, I was surprised at the sheer turnout. And I'd say, this is actually lively, I go, this is actually something good ... that actually inspired me ... It's something different. I started getting the hang of it ... and then all of a sudden ... I'm at every meeting and I'm helping out. I'm getting the inside information out and ... I'm trying to be a GMB rep. (Global Majority worker-leader GA-18)

Organizers identified some key moments as turning points in the workers' growing confidence, to exert power in making the picket an autonomous time and space. These included:

- the first arrival of police at the picket, which initially prompted the workers to fall silent and move on to the pavement, until a Somali man took the megaphone and walked up the line of workers saying that the police were 'in Amazon's pocket', after which people stepped back into the road one by one;
- an incident in which the police stopped a Ghanaian worker's car and performed a vehicle check next to the picket, provoking workers to come together across ethnicities and protest in solidarity;
- the demand from an Eritrean woman picketer that GMB organizers must take action to remove an Amazon manager who had come

out to visibly film the striking workers, which organizers were successful in doing – this reportedly marked a shift in the workers' ownership of the pickets and confidence to make demands of organizers.[26]

At a later stage in the campaign, I witnessed this confidence of workers to challenge authority figures, recording in my picket fieldnotes:

> Police sergeant referred to [a] car that had stopped for a long time and people talking to the driver as 'idiots', was challenged directly by multiple workers demanding he be professional and pointing out his wages [are] paid by taxes paid by them ... [the sergeant] retreated down the street.[27]

Organizers reported that they thought the police were probably avoiding any direct confrontation because they did not want the publicity of being seen defending Amazon. This highlights the importance of the GMB's longstanding work, alongside many other organizations, to raise public awareness of Amazon's practices through media engagement and promoting awareness of workers' stories, which could be seen as a form of discursive power.[28]

There was also evidence that these strikes built workers' confidence to contest the space of the warehouse during working hours, with reports from worker-leaders and organizers suggesting a growing culture of formal and informal resistance as the unionization process continued. A worker-leader expressed the confident use of formal grievance processes:

> For union representatives and workplace leaders, I urge vigilance. Document everything, involve witnesses, and whenever possible, raise grievances as a group to ensure fair hearings. Many people aren't aware but under Amazon's Grievance Policy, if a grievance is raised as a group, then it will be heard as a group. Do not let them divide and conquer, as that is a tactic that they often deploy ... Together, we can work towards an environment where equal opportunity, respect and integrity are upheld. Most importantly, we need to

> remember that change starts with us and that we are in
> this together. (Global Majority worker-leader GA-16)

This expresses a clear orientation towards using formal company policies to build worker power. In an example of the kind of informal resistance that was also encouraged by this growing confidence among workers, a wildcat stoppage was staged for two hours in the Transportation Operations Management (TOM) team to prevent the transfer of seven workers to less favourable roles within the warehouse, and this was followed by a successful collective grievance in the same department later in the year.[29]

Having built membership to a sufficient level through strikes, the GMB applied for formal recognition in March 2024. The CAC judged that there was sufficient evidence of majority support for the union to grant a ballot of the workforce. While this is discussed further in Chapter 4, in the context of this chapter, it is important to note that the ballot enabled organizers to have more direct access to workers within the warehouse, albeit for a brief 'access period' prior to the vote, and the union maximized this opportunity to reach more of the workforce. Together with notice boards and screens displaying union material, which Amazon were forced to allow under the terms of the ballot, the GMB held meetings within the warehouse that were open to all workers. These meetings took a participatory approach, including an exercise where workers were invited to write issues that were of concern to them on a sheet on the wall, and then to vote on those issues that were the highest priority, followed by time for open discussion.[30] The union also offered drop-in sessions, although under the terms of the access agreement, these took place during workers' already very limited break times and were therefore poorly attended. Furthermore, all of this access to the space of the warehouse was under close supervision by Amazon, with security guards reportedly directed to go as far as accompanying organizers on trips to the toilet.[31]

Alongside strikes and the application for recognition, workers also made extensive use of Amazon's own structures to reach other workers within the space of the warehouse – for example, its 'Voice of the Associates' (VOA) online message board, meetings convened by Amazon such as 'Team Connects', 'Shift Briefings' and 'All-Hands Meetings', and the delegate Associate Forum.[32] The latter was made up of Associates, and Amazon argues that this provides its employees with a voice that negates the need for a trade union. Yet the GMB worker-leaders at BHX4 included multiple people who had tried to support their colleagues as part of the Associate Forum and had reached the conclusion that it was ineffectual because it lacked power, did not afford Forum members any right to speak when accompanying workers to formal meetings, and was easily ignored by management. This is illustrated by the following worker-leader's comments:

> I feel first hand, like they [managers] say: 'OK, if you [have] got issues with management or HR, talk to your Forum' ... But reality is, we can log it down, it gets pushed back ... so we [are] getting brushed under the carpet ... All we do when we listen to [workers, as an Associate Forum member], we go, we understand them, we want to help them, unfortunately our hands are tied. We cannot do anything because of the role we're given. All we're going to do is give feedback to them at the end of the day ... and every Associate Forum member will tell you this, we can only accompany you ... we're not allowed to speak ... I can't protect you ... I can only sit there ... feel sorry for you ... to take whatever punishment they get. And I can't do nothing for you. But GMB rep, they're going to fight it. (Global Majority worker-leader GA-18)

While Associate Forum members in the GMB were clear that they did not use their Forum role to directly organize for the union, this role gave them extensive contacts and a profile with workers across different departments that they may not otherwise have had. Meanwhile, the VOA board was accessible to all workers and became an intense battleground, particularly in the period leading up to the July 2024 recognition ballot. Although union leaders complained that their VOA posts were regularly deleted by management, a worker-leader gave the following example of using the VOA board to get clarification from managers in writing in front of the whole workforce, in a context where worker-leaders had heard that managers were spreading rumours that recognition could lead the warehouse to close:

[W]e put [it] on the VOA board and ask … our new General Manager: 'Is it true that if we get recognition, you're going to close the FC? [fulfilment centre]' So that we hold it to his word and he said it coherently that they are not, even though recognition happens in the FC, they are not closing the FC. (Global Majority worker-leader GA-33)

In another example of how these internal systems were used, within hours of the recognition ballot result, a worker-leader posted the following message on the VOA Board, signalling to workers that the struggle was not over:

Dear Colleagues,

Let this be a moment to regroup and strengthen our resolve. Your bravery in standing up for your rights remains crucial, and it is essential to maintain this momentum. Use this experience to continue advocating for positive change, knowing that the fight for fair treatment and better work conditions is ongoing. Together we will keep pushing forward, learning from this experience, and striving towards a future where every worker's voice is heard and respected.

Workers in roles that afforded them mobility around the workplace and contact with a range of workers also played a crucial role. This highlights the value in using all possible structures afforded by the workplace to reach workers.

Overall, reaching the whole workforce at BHX4 was highly challenging because of the systematic fragmentation of labour produced by Amazon's organization of the time and space of the warehouse. The GMB's successes in overcoming these challenges combined periods of slow preparation and rapid acceleration, and the use of all existing spaces, together with the creation of new autonomous spaces, through strike time, which enabled workers and organizers to move more freely. This in turn opened up new spaces within the warehouse, as workers built confidence and practical skills to assert influence in defence of their interests. Reaching the whole workforce was thus chiefly about working creatively with time and space to enable workers whose movement Amazon sought to control to come together under their own autonomous direction, even briefly, to form relationships of solidarity. Such tactics supplement McAlevey's general points about worker democracy (see Chapter 2) because they show how democratic organizing can be enacted even in a tightly controlled workplace with a highly diverse and residentially dispersed workforce.

This has wide relevance given that the vast majority of workers in the UK and many other countries are not organized, work in fragmented environments and face an array of different immediate issues, and in many cases worsening conditions of precarity.[33] It is often difficult or impossible to predict where and when moments of spontaneous collectivity will emerge. Yet, the GMB's work at BHX4 demonstrates that consistent groundwork to build contacts and trust can provide a strong foundation on which to respond quickly to sudden developments, and shows how this can be further developed by finding ways to create spaces and times for autonomous association.

Reflective questions for organizers, worker-leaders and activists

- What were the main challenges for the GMB to reach the whole workforce at BHX4?
- How were these challenges addressed?
- What challenges do you face reaching the whole workforce in your organizing?
- How do you address this and how could you further improve?

Notes

[1] Gall, G. (2005) 'Organizing non-union workers as trade unionists in the "new economy" in Britain', *Economic and Industrial Democracy*, 26(1): 41–63; Sadler, J. (2012) 'The importance of multiple leadership roles in fostering participation', *Leadership & Organization Development Journal*, 33(8): 779–796.

[2] GMB (2024) 'Make Work Better: GMB workplace representatives and shop stewards induction course, part 1 (Autumn 2024–Summer 2025 ed.)', p 26.

[3] Fieldnotes 9 January 2024.

[4] Fieldnotes 7 February 2024.

[5] Fieldnotes 13 March 2024.

[6] GMB (n 2), p 26.

[7] Fieldnotes 24 April 2024.

[8] *New York Times*, 2021, [online], Available from: https://www.nytimes.com/interactive/2021/06/15/us/amazon-workers.html [Accessed 15 May 2025].

[9] Office for National Statistics (ONS) (2022) 'Consumer price inflation, UK: August 2022', [online], Available from: https://www.ons.gov.uk/economy/inflationandpriceindices/bulletins/consumerpriceinflation/august2022 [Accessed 12 November 2024].

[10] Fieldnotes 17 September 2024.

[11] Kassem, S. (2023) *Work and Alienation in the Platform Economy: Amazon and the Power of Organisation*, Bristol: Bristol University Press, p 88.

[12] Kassem (n 11); Boyle, K.A. (2024) 'The discursive power of trade union leadership: framing identity fields for public persuasion', *Work, Employment and Society*, DOI:10.1177/09500170241279778.

[13] Interview GA-03.

[14] Fieldnotes 19 December 2024.

[15] McAlevey, J.F. (2023) *Rules to Win By: Power and Participation in Union Negotiations*, Oxford: Oxford University Press, pp 45–47.

[16] Vgontzas, N. (2020) 'A new industrial working class? Challenges in disrupting Amazon's fulfillment process in Germany', in J. Alimahomed-Wilson and E. Reese (eds) *The Cost of Free Shipping: Amazon in the Global Economy*, London: Pluto Press, pp 116–128.

[17] Boewe, J. and Schulten, J. (2020) 'Amazon strikes in Europe: seven years of industrial action, challenges, and strategies', in J. Alimahomed-Wilson and E. Reese (eds) *The Cost of Free Shipping: Amazon in the Global Economy*, London: Pluto Press, pp 209–224.

[18] Gall (n 1), p 53.

[19] Holgate, J. (2021) *Arise: Power, Strategy and Union Resurgence*, London: Pluto Press.

[20] Interview GA-06.

[21] GMB (n 2), p 26.

[22] Fieldnotes 5 June 2024.

[23] Fieldnotes 13 February 2024.

[24] Fieldnotes 24 April 2024.

[25] Fieldnotes 13 February 2024.

[26] Fieldnotes 19 December 2023.

[27] Fieldnotes 14 February 2024.

[28] Boyle (n 12).

[29] Fieldnotes 25 January 2024; personal communication GA-06.

[30] Fieldnotes 18 June 2024.

[31] Fieldnotes 17 September 2024.

[32] Fieldnotes 9 January 2024, 7 February 2024, 13 March 2024.

[33] Vickers, T. (2019) *Borders, Migration and Class: Producing Immigrants and Workers*, Bristol: Bristol University Press.

ESSAY 3

How Amazon Tried to Persuade Workers Against the Union

Louveza Iqbal, GMB worker-leader at BHX4

When we first started talking about seeking union recognition within our workplace, a sense of hope arose among all workers. It made us feel like we could have a voice and finally be heard. For years we have been actively campaigning and fighting, so it was our time to rise up. All we wanted was to be treated fairly, with respect and not made to feel like slaves.

Our fight was to be paid fairly. We demanded £15 an hour because it's disgusting that the biggest e-commerce company in the world has been paying their workers the bare minimum, whereas other, less profitable companies pay their employees much more. As a result, we went on multiple strikes.

However, Amazon did everything they could to stop workers from striking. For example, on strike days, Amazon managers would incentivize workers to come into work with food vouchers. They stood at the entrance in the morning and handed £2.50 food vouchers to anyone who chose to work that day instead of striking. I found this incredibly shocking, because I have spoken to many workers who work the entire ten-hour shift on an empty stomach. Many workers at Amazon come with their families from abroad. They spend money on rent, bills, buses to and from work, and they send a lot of money back home too. As a result, it means many workers are living paycheck to paycheck and have little money for essentials such as heating and food. Amazon knows this and used it as a tool to help their anti-union agenda. It's really sickening that Amazon only helps their starving workers when it benefits them.

Unfortunately, throughout this entire process Amazon unleashed a wave of dirty tactics to manipulate their workers and keep them in line.

At first, it began with simple things such as posters being plastered everywhere – from leaflets on the canteen tables, posters in bathroom stalls, PowerPoint displays on every screen. Anti-union propaganda was everywhere and you couldn't avoid it

Soon after, they launched phase two of their anti-union campaign. They organized 'voluntary' information sessions where a manager read off a script designed to brainwash us. They told us that unions would take our money, make decisions for us or even cause our FC to close. This was a clear attempt to manipulate, confuse and frighten us. I attended several of these brainwashing meetings and every time I would be forced to call out and challenge the managers on the lies they were spewing. Considering English isn't the first language for the majority of workers here, it would be easy to confuse them. Amazon knew this and they capitalized on employees' weaknesses for their own gain.

Amazon used every trick in the book, from constantly observing us (especially pro-union workers) to spreading lies and rumours. They tried to divide us, to scare us, to silence us, but it only made us more committed and determined. Sure, Amazon has millions of pounds to pump into their anti-union campaign, but we had something worth much more. We have a collective spirit, a strong drive to win and a relentless will to fight for what we deserve. We may have barely lost, by a marginal number, due to Amazon's anti-union campaign, but we will always have the motivation and desire to be treated with dignity and to win!

ESSAY 4

Stopping, Watching and Listening: The Importance of Mindfulness for Organizing

Rachel Fagan, GMB Regional Organizer

When the wildcat walkouts started in August 2022, GMB members working at BHX4 knew what to do. The years leading up to this had instilled in them the relationship with the GMB Union and an understanding of what it meant to be a member.

We were told that workers would gather in Coventry city centre to protest; they felt used by Amazon and wanted the world to know. Workers began to walk out of the site and started to hold their own protests, creating their own signs and chants, calling for better pay and working conditions.

We listened to what these workers wanted. It was clear that they wanted to tell their story about what it was like to work for this global giant and what they had had to go through during the COVID-19 pandemic that secured Amazon profits. Workers were furious that Amazon had not shared the wealth with the workforce that had created it. They wanted to protest and they wanted to be heard.

We had to step back and be in that moment, to look and listen. Who was the person that others were going to? Who was organizing all the workers? Who was handing out signs? Who was leading the chants? Who was talking to other people? Because these were the people that we needed to engage with first. So, we went to them, and we listened to them and empathized with them; a few we knew were already GMB members, but the majority of workers that had started to protest were not members of the union, but felt so strongly about what they were fighting for. It was at that point that we realized we needed to capture those workers, and with pen and paper, we went through the crowds asking everybody for their name and phone number so we could set up the WhatsApp groups. We knew that we would never have the opportunity to speak to these workers face to face again and needed to enable the conversation to continue.

There followed picket lines and mass demonstrations on the driveway leading into BHX4, mass group meetings that were attended by over 1,000 workers. It was important that throughout the campaign, we kept the fire burning, meaning the agitation, the drive, the opportunity to speak and for your voice to be heard. It was important that at all stages, the workers understood the key messaging and next steps. Industrial action played a key part in enabling us to speak to, and consult face to face with, members – as an organizer, the members are the most precious resource you can have. The dispute did what Amazon hated – it brought together the workforce and removed the divides that Amazon had worked so hard to put in place. The dispute created a space to engage, it overcame the barrier of access to the workforce and we used every single moment of it to build and organize.

Building relationships was a fundamental part of this campaign. This was not just about being contactable, but being relatable, supportive and reactive. Relationships we have forged with the membership at BHX4 created the 'GMB Family'. These key contacts with members range between a WhatsApp chat where workers have an opportunity to feed into what matters most to them, a phone call to check that they've returned a ballot paper, or a meeting for the communication action networks to make key strategic decisions.

Throughout the entire campaign, it was important to show workers that we were there and we weren't going anywhere. We had a constant presence outside the gates of BHX4, whether it be to distribute a new flyer, counteracting Amazon's union-busting or placards saying 'Vote Yes for Hope', 'Vote Yes for Dignity', 'Vote Yes for Respect'. This was particularly important when we got the results of the failed recognition ballot, and what a testament to these workers, their enthusiasm, drive and engagement on that day to truly show that this fight was not over.

The true success of this campaign will always be a unionized workplace. And this is what we've achieved: workers who understand the worth and strength of the collective. The Amazon Workers' Branch is a functioning and supportive hub of trained GMB health and safety representatives. All of this has been achieved without statutory access, facility time, and despite all the barriers a company like Amazon could throw at it. This shows how key it was to be mindful of the time and moments we had to engage with workers, making sure that every second counted to create a unionized and organized workplace.

4

Sustaining Action and Engagement

As Sadler argues, unions' 'biggest assets are the volume of people, their members' willingness to voluntarily participate in union activities, and their members' collective ingenuity'.[1] Consequently, securing and maintaining voluntary participation is crucial to union success. This is expressed in the GMB organizing principle that: 'Each workplace should be organised as if a ballot for action was due.'[2] In a case like Amazon, where there are numerous issues that many workers feel must be addressed, a sustained process of change-oriented action is called for. This chapter examines the challenges that were encountered at BHX4 in sustaining action and engagement, followed by the GMB's response.

Challenges in sustaining action and engagement

This section begins by discussing migrants' social and legal position in Britain, which produced distinct patterns of precarity and limitations on rights within the BHX4 workforce and consequently created challenges for sustained union engagement. Discussion then moves on to financial barriers to sustained action, which were exacerbated by the unequal spatial relations of global capitalism that made many workers' families reliant on the money they sent home. This is followed by a discussion of the impact of British legislation governing strikes on workers who were not yet familiar with British institutions. The section concludes with a review of Amazon's direct attempts to disrupt and curtail union activity at BHX4, which relied on the company's near-total monopoly control over the space of the warehouse and workers' time within it.

I have previously shown that migrants' disadvantaged position in the British labour market has multiple causes, but is ultimately rooted in the unequal spatial arrangements of global capitalism.[3] These international relations are reflected in the super-exploitation of workers who move to Britain from less powerful countries and are further reinforced by the immigration policies of the British state. The varying conditions of exploitation that migrants face also have a temporal dimension, including situations in which some migrants become 'stuck', unable to access work or move on from jobs that are harmful, and in other cases conditions of enforced speed, such as the pressure to move regularly in search of work or to juggle multiple jobs simultaneously.[4] This presented several challenges to sustained action by BHX4 workers, who had a wide array of immigration statuses, from refugees to dependants on a partner's visa, to international students and people on work visas. The precarious and conditional nature of such immigration statuses made some workers more dependent on their employer and more fearful of challenging mistreatment or joining a union,[5] as well as subjecting them to hefty fees for visas, the Immigration Health Surcharge and chargeable National Health Service (NHS) treatments.[6] The variety of immigration situations among the workforce was a further source of fragmentation, making it harder to identify shared immediate issues.

A further challenge in sustaining action was financial, as workers' low wages combined with family members' reliance on their remittances. As one Eritrean worker put it while gesturing to his colleagues on the picket line: 'Everyone here is supporting at least three people back home.'[7] This increased the risks for workers if they were to lose their job as a result of victimization for trade union activity, or even to have a temporary disruption to income as a result of reduced hours or strike action.[8] Given these economic insecurities and family dependencies, it would have been extremely difficult if not impossible for many BHX4 workers to strike without significant hardship payments from the union. Even with hardship payments, worker-leaders reported some members struggling with the net reduction to their income after taking into account lost earnings due to strikes, the level of hardship payments and union membership fees.[9] Some workers cited friends who could not afford to strike, and one worker told me they could only manage by working extra hours as a Just Eat delivery driver during Amazon strike days.[10]

As well as the financial pressures involved in sustaining strike action, UK legislation imposed a periodic barrier in the form of a postal strike ballot. Striking was a preferred tactic among a large section of the workforce and, as discussed earlier, brought multiple benefits in terms of creating a time and space for the free association of workers beyond Amazon's control. However, striking with legal protections in the UK at that time required a postal ballot with a minimum turnout of 50 per cent of members to produce a six-month strike mandate. Maintaining an ongoing process of periodic strikes, as favoured by GMB members at BHX4, therefore required repeated postal ballots to maintain the strike mandate, each time passing the 50 per cent turnout threshold. This is a challenging hurdle under any circumstances – one that my own University and College Union (UCU) branch has often failed to pass. This has also proven a significant barrier for Amazon workers in other countries – for example, in Poland, a ballot for strike action in 2016 mobilized 2,150 workers across the two sites of Wrocław and Poznań, but was insufficient to produce a strike mandate because this fell below the minimum 50 per cent turnout required by law.[11]

Reaching the legal threshold was made harder at BHX4 by workers' lack of familiarity with British institutions, not only regarding their rights at work and legal protections for trade union activity but also knowledge of how to use the postal system, which was the only means allowed by the state to participate in strike ballots. Furthermore, organizers and worker-leaders reported that many BHX4 workers lived in shared accommodation where postal ballots could easily get lost, had frequent changes of address due to housing insecurity, which required regular monitoring and updating of records to ensure that the addresses held by the union for balloting were accurate, and/or struggled to find time to get to a post box around long hours of work and childcare, with some parents working alternate shifts so that one parent was home with the children while the other was in the warehouse.[12]

Sustaining action was further challenged by direct interventions by Amazon management and HR (human resources department). The following account expresses the longstanding climate of fear and curtailment of worker voice within the warehouse:

> [T]he little posters in the toilets [saying] 'Come and speak
> to us [managers]. You don't need to pay to speak to [us,
> unlike] a union. You can come, our doors are always
> open.' I've known people go in those doors, speak to
> managers and not come back. People know the limits
> of what they can say to managers. (European worker-
> leader GA-02)

More particularly, worker-leaders reported widespread fear among
workers of being victimized by Amazon for trade union activity,
which they described as being shaped by several distinct phases in
Amazon's response to unionization.

In the first phase, when the level of unionization at BHX4 was still
low, leaders described direct pressure from Amazon to not discuss
the union with workmates, and worker-leaders being removed from
certain roles or receiving reduced hours if they were on a flexible
contract. Intimidation was also reported during the first official strike,
as the following worker-leader described:

> [A]t the start, they were very strict and it was like ... if I'm
> talking to you about the union ... I'll be into a meeting
> with a disciplinary, just for mentioning the word union.
> But obviously, because the GMB's turned around and
> said: 'If they try, that's a protected characteristic [under
> the UK's Equality Act] and we're gonna protect you.'
> ... But I think the problem is trying to explain that to
> a new non-English person. Because they hear it from a
> manager. (European worker-leader GA-04)

Despite this intimidation, worker-leaders persisted in their
recruitment of colleagues, using a combination of the kind of support
from organizers described earlier and creative use of spaces within
the warehouse such as smoking shelters and a QR code on the back
of worker-leaders' phones to enable quick recruitment of colleagues
without attracting managers' attention.

In the second phase, as union membership rose, workers described
less opposition from managers. Some interviewees linked this to
Amazon's experience of the unionization battle at its Staten Island site
in the US, where the sacking of union leader Chris Smalls prompted

a reaction by workers that resulted in the site becoming the first unionized Amazon warehouse in the country. Yet even during this period, worker-leaders reported that Amazon maintained a steady pressure to dissuade BHX4 workers from joining a union: 'Amazon as well campaigned against GMB, even though they will say "Oh, we accept your right to join any union", but they still work in between to tell you that joining a union won't give you the best option' (Global Majority worker-leader GA-05). Such subtle opposition was clearly insufficient, as GMB membership continued to rise.

In a third phase, after the GMB applied for formal union recognition in March 2024, Amazon reportedly went on the offensive. Worker-leaders told me about threats made to them by managers during this period. For example, a worker-leader who had secured a change of role after collapsing at work and suffering ongoing health problems said that a manager told them following the application for recognition that they should be grateful for the accommodations that had been made due to their health, and threatened them by saying: 'You want equality, do you want me to put you back in the line?'[13] The phrase 'in the line' here refers to a physically demanding role on the packing line. This was reportedly followed by a different manager telling the same worker-leader that their occupational health accommodations would be reviewed. When the ballot commenced, they were indeed transferred back into the line, after which they again collapsed and were taken to hospital by ambulance. They reported that the Chair of the Associate Forum told them that the reason they had been transferred back into the line was that their previous role was seen as giving them too much opportunity to speak with colleagues.[14]

In the period leading up to the ballot, weeks before the GMB had access to the BHX4 warehouse, worker-leaders reported that at least 30 Amazon managers were drafted in from other sites across the UK. They were described as talking to workers on the line, as well as in dedicated meetings, and sometimes following worker-leaders around trying to persuade them against the union while they tried to do their job. A worker-leader stated that 'we have external managers coming in, speaking to the staff for the last few weeks … And then [saying], why you shouldn't join GMB, "What's there for you?", "You're going to lose a benefit", "GMB can't do nothing for you", [and] so on' (Global Majority worker-leader GA-18).

Worker-leaders said that it was particularly noticeable that some of these managers were of the same nationalities as some of the largest sections of the workforce, and for the first time in these worker-leaders' experience Amazon held meetings and produced written information in workers' first languages, all directly arguing against union recognition.[15] Worker-leaders described how:

> [O]ne month before [the recognition ballot], and they even started to bring their different managers from other FCs. Because when they find out … a majority of them … working [in the warehouse are] Indians, OK, in what language [do] they speak? For example, if they speak Telugu, they try to bring them managers from Telugu. When they find out the Punjabi … they bring the managers from Punjabi … and for the Eritreans also working [in] most [large numbers], so they try to bring that the guy who can speak their language. And also … one of the managers speaking Arabic … So, they tried to brainwash the people as much as possible. (Global Majority worker-leader GA-32)

Another worker-leader confirmed the role of these external managers in trying to persuade workers against voting for recognition:

> 90 per cent of Eritreans are GMB members. I think there's 90 per cent of Ethiopians that are GMB members as well. Majority of that culture, they speak the same language. What [Amazon have] done, out of the blue, they've called in a manager from London that speaks the language… I've been watching this guy … I'm on my line, I'm talking to another [member of staff] … This guy comes past, he ignores me. Talks to him [another worker] in his own language … Then … he's on the next line. And he's talking to everybody … I ask someone: 'Look, who is he?' They go: 'Oh yeah, he's talking about GMB, why you don't want to join.' (Global Majority worker-leader GA-18)

Each worker was invited to as many as five or more hour-long meetings, described as 'voluntary information sessions', held by

Amazon to argue against recognition, prior to the union's access period, and further meetings in between the end of the period allowed for GMB meetings and the opening of the ballot. The following worker-leaders described how:

> [L]eading to the ballot, the organizing was not really fair, because Amazon had their several meetings … it was supposed to be 45 minutes … Even some persons even had like four or five meetings. (Global Majority worker-leader GA-33)

> GMB session, they gave only 45 minutes, but the Amazon session … went up to … two hours… they have that money and … it is their company. So, they spend all of the hours, they don't even care about [whether] the Associates are working or not. (Global Majority worker-leader GA-32)

The reference to Amazon's ability to 'spend all of the hours' in order to persuade workers emphasizes the importance of control over time and space in the struggle for ideological supremacy. A worker-leader suggested that many workers attended the voluntary Amazon sessions simply as an opportunity to have a rest from their exhausting work,[16] highlighting Amazon's ability to manipulate workers' movements. This was combined with the use of management structures such as 'Team Connects', to bombard workers with information that created a climate of fear about the possible consequences of recognition:

> [T]he lies Amazon has fed them about losing their jobs, about the closure of the FC, has really been a big challenge for us … Amazon has already fed them with the lies and the managers calling them all of a sudden in Connect meetings and telling them how they are going to close the FC. (Global Majority worker-leader GA-33)

The following worker-leader further described the fear created by Amazon's interventions:

> They [management] organize a meeting with people
> to say what [is] bad is [the] union … And they send
> rumours. For instance, if the union come here, we'll
> close. And the people are scared … they come to me …
> to all representatives, they said … they can't close the
> warehouse. (European migrant worker-leader GA-21)

Amid this climate of uncertainty, BHX4 management promoted the
message that voting 'No' was the safest course, summed up in slogans
such as the following, displayed inside the warehouse on screens and
posters during the ballot:

> Not sure if you want GMB to gain recognition? Don't sit
> on the fence. You can vote no to keep your options open.
>
> GMB makes promises. Amazon delivers progress. Vote
> for Amazon guarantees over union unknowns.

Anti-union propaganda was displayed throughout the warehouse on
screens, pop-up stands, displays on every table in the canteen, and the
backs of toilet stall doors. This echoed the company's response to the
first attempt to formally unionize an Amazon warehouse in the US, in
Bessemer, Alabama, where workers narrowly lost the vote after facing
an anti-union campaign that included 'a website, plastering even toilet
stalls with anti-union flyers, and mobilising worker "ambassadors"
to express anti-union sentiment on social media'.[17] Organizers
reported that they counted a greater number of Amazon's anti-union
noticeboards, screens and signs just in the entrance corridor to BHX4
than the GMB was allowed to display in the entire building during
the access period.[18] Some of these anti-union materials included a
QR code that workers could use to generate an email from their own
account to the GMB cancelling their membership – a measure that the
union responded to with a legal claim, alleging that this constituted
a service that was an inducement to leave the union.[19]

The barriers to sustained action at BHX4 were therefore multiple
and intersecting. In particular, many workers' limited knowledge
about UK rights and institutions and their financial commitments
to family overseas made it easier for Amazon to create uncertainty
about what the consequences of recognition might be, and the

risk that it might destabilize their continued ability to earn. The GMB responded to this through a constantly evolving practice in and around the workplace that used the union's financial resources to create temporary spaces for autonomous movement while also educating workers and using legal and political mechanisms to further enlarge this space.

The GMB's response to sustain action and engagement

This section explores the GMB's assertion of space for workers to continue taking action. This included diverse means of communication that were outside of Amazon's control and hardship payments that reduced workers' reliance on Amazon's wages, thereby freeing them to some extent from the conditional form of mobility-as-labour that Amazon imposed. The attempt to further contest Amazon's control within the warehouse by institutionalizing the union's presence via an application for recognition is also discussed.

After an early strike ballot in which the union narrowly failed to reach the 50 per cent turnout threshold, worker-leaders insisted they could win a reballot and the GMB adopted a number of new measures, learning from the experience of the failed ballot. One organizer explained:

> I was reluctant to go for a second ballot ... I thought, 'I don't think I could go through all that again and lose at the end of it'. But ... a [worker] leader said: 'No, we're going to do more. We were a bit complacent, we're going to do more.' And we had a bit of a review on what we'd done wrong. (European organizer GA-09)

New measures included changes to the materials accompanying ballot papers, making creative use of the options allowed under the rules. While the ballot papers had to be dispatched by a third party, Civica, which limited the GMB's direct involvement, organizers discovered they could specify the colour of the envelope and include an insert giving information in multiple languages. They used the union's primary colour of orange and advised members to look out for the orange envelope, even going as far as producing a giant orange cardboard envelope as a visual aid to help explain to workers at the gate what they should be looking for. Union materials were initially distributed in extensive written translation, but through feedback from worker-leaders, a more effective strategy was developed using QR codes leading to translated videos, visual leaflets with pictures of ballot envelopes and post boxes, and voicenotes circulated via WhatsApp. Over time, the work of translation was taken over by workers themselves, and by September 2024, the union was routinely producing audio and video translations in 13 languages.[20] Numerous 'gate jobs' were held, during which organizers and worker-leaders explained about the ballot and distributed fliers as workers entered the building, accompanied by phone banking sessions in which worker-leaders phoned and texted other members, later supplemented by 'peer-to-peer' texting software provided by the TUC. Where members could not be reached by phone, worker-leaders and organizers visited their homes. The personnel required for this extensive work was supplemented by GMB worker-leaders from a range of other sectors – including teaching assistants, care staff, refuse workers and call centre operatives – who were undertaking a paid scholarship programme, the Midlands School of Organising, whereby they were seconded to the GMB full-time for a period of six months to develop their organizing skills.

The GMB took direct action to mitigate financial barriers to strike action by issuing hardship payments of £70 per day, which is significantly higher than most unions offer in the UK, if such payments are made at all. Workers were held accountable for these payments by a requirement to attend a two-hour picket shift in either the morning or evening of each strike day, with attendance monitored by systems for signing in and signing out. Again, this is highly unusual for a British trade union; the practice had been adopted in the region following its success in a previous dispute with another company, GKN, the leader of which had since become a paid GMB organizer who was now involved in the Amazon campaign.[21] With pickets across shifts that often involved more than 1,000 people per day and 37 days of strike action within two years, these hardship payments amounted to a very considerable sum of money. An organizer expressed the importance of these payments, but also the role they played in limiting strike action to what could be afforded, arguing that 'it's an enabler, in that it allows you to get workers at very low pay ... to come out and take strike action, but ... it restricts you because where's the money for it coming from' (European organizer GA-06). While some important fundraising was contributed by other trade union branches and individual supporters, which will be discussed further later on, most of this money came from GMB regional funds. This reflects a high degree of commitment by senior regional officials to the strategic importance of Amazon for the future of work. It also highlights the benefits of a large and well-established trade union supporting precarious and low-paid workers to take action.

The prospect of securing formal recognition offered the GMB several benefits for the sustainability of unionization at BHX4, as well as increased powers. The GMB first applied for recognition at BHX4 in 2023, but withdrew its application after Amazon recruited 1,100 additional workers in a short period, significantly diluting the union membership below the 50 per cent support required for recognition. A worker-leader explained that 'they've just hired up loads more people that they haven't really needed. They've not needed all these people because half of them are standing around doing nothing' (European worker-leader GA-04).

Worker-leaders reported that this increase in staffing also led to a reduction in offers of overtime. Because many of the new workers were on temporary contracts, the GMB then filed another application with the bargaining unit defined as Level One Associates on permanent contracts, at which point organizers said that Amazon made many of the temporary workers permanent. After a further period of strikes and recruitment, the GMB again filed for recognition in March 2024, in response to which the CAC granted a ballot, which the union ultimately lost following the massive anti-union campaign by Amazon described earlier in this chapter.

Although specific details would depend on the recognition agreement, fundamentally recognition would have required Amazon to negotiate over pay, hours and holiday for all workers within the bargaining unit, increasing the power of workers to contest the scheduling and reward for their work. It would also usually be expected to include a system for electing health and safety representatives and arrangements for the union to have a consistent presence on site, which might be facilitated, for example, by a union office, paid 'facility time' for elected union representatives, and access to the building by organizers. This would have created protected space within the warehouse for the union and strengthened workers' power to contest Amazon's control of workers' mobile bodies by monitoring the consequences for their health and safety. Some worker-leaders expressed the sense of confidence that recognition would have given them and other workers, because having organizers within the workplace would make them feel a stronger connection to the wider union: 'I think [the] union will be strong, in my opinion, if we'll be inside [by having recognition] … everything will be different … When the people see the recognition they see there … you have a link' (European migrant worker-leader GA-21). This expresses a weaving together, or 'link', between the space of the warehouse and the wider spatial extent of the national union, and a fundamental shift in the spatial dynamics of the warehouse by having the union 'inside'.

Recognition would also have helped extend the unionization drive to other sites, as an organizer explained: 'it's something we can hold up and say "Look, we've got recognition", and also that may help that to spread into other regions that might say "It's possible"' (European organizer GA-09).

At the same time, some organizers clearly expressed the limitations of the recognition process, arguing that recognition should not be seen as an end in itself, but merely one means to consolidate the position of the workers and their leaders. An organizer highlighted some of the contradictory consequences of formal recognition:

> Recognition is not going to be the be all and end all of BHX4, it's going to make it a lot more difficult. [If the GMB get recognition] they're [Amazon] going to try and play them [BHX4 workers] off against other sites. They're going to try and put structures in place that create hierarchy, that will create division within the rep structures. They'll try and put people on full time facilities [released full time from Amazon work for union duties], which … I'm dead against because … [as] soon as you take somebody off the tools, you deskill them in … how they communicate with the workforce. So, there's … a big road that's going to need to be navigated. (European organizer GA-08)

Another organizer emphasized that they were attempting to use the campaign for recognition to build worker leadership, in contrast to its frequent role encouraging member passivity:

> [A] lot of unionized workplaces with recognition actually have low [membership] density, low member engagement, don't have any of the things that we're trying to achieve ... What we're trying to do at Amazon is ... we're trying to get Amazon workers themselves to represent people as union reps, rather than the union coming in from the outside. (European organizer GA-06)

This demonstrated a high level of awareness among organizers that formal recognition carries with it significant dangers, including the potential for the institutionalization of the union's presence within the warehouse to have the unintended consequence of separating worker-leaders from the rest of the workforce and replacing their organic leadership with paid officers.

Alongside this collective action around strikes and the campaign for recognition, representation of individual members in BHX4 played an important role in sustaining membership by winning some important victories that spread by word of mouth to other workers and encouraged them to join the GMB and maintain their membership. This representation was initially undertaken exclusively by paid organizers, but was increasingly replaced by reps among the worker-leaders,[22] who had been trained through the process that will be described in Chapter 5.

Overall, sustaining action and engagement at BHX4 relied fundamentally on struggles over time and space: sustaining legal protections for strike time through ballots that were won through a sophisticated communications strategy; providing financial support so that workers could claim the autonomy of a strike free from the conditional mobility imposed by an Amazon wage while still meeting their obligations to family; and, finally, by the attempt to institutionalize the GMB's presence within the warehouse through formal recognition imposed on Amazon by the CAC.

The lessons of this experience have broad relevance because the UK's legal framework makes it extremely hard to win a formal strike ballot, particularly among highly precarious, large and divided workforces. Yet the BHX4 experience shows that this can be done and how this was achieved. Furthermore, it demonstrates the benefits that can result from strategic deployment of a large union's resources in terms of financially supporting sustained action by precarious and low-paid workers. Sustaining engagement through a programme of active confrontation with the employer has important implications for members' understanding of the nature of the union as a vehicle for struggle. At BHX4, this engendered a sense of political purpose that Holgate argues British trade unions have often lacked, but which she argues was also evident in Unite the Union's Community membership.[23] Lastly, the BHX4 experience highlights the difficulties securing formal recognition against a large and wealthy employer that takes a stance of determined opposition, and the potential benefits and risks if recognition were won.

Reflective questions for organizers, worker-leaders and activists

- What were the main challenges for the GMB to sustain action and engagement at BHX4?
- How were these challenges addressed?
- What challenges do you face sustaining action and engagement in your organizing?
- How do you address these challenges and how could you further improve?

Notes

[1] Sadler, J. (2012) 'The importance of multiple leadership roles in fostering participation', *Leadership & Organization Development Journal*, 33(8): 779–796, at 779.

[2] GMB (2024) 'Make Work Better: GMB workplace representatives and shop stewards induction course, part 1 (Autumn 2024–Summer 2025 ed.)', p 26.

[3] Vickers, T. (2019) *Borders, Migration and Class: Producing Immigrants and Workers*, Bristol: Bristol University Press.

[4] Vickers (n 3); Datta, K., McIlwaine, C., Evans, Y., Herbert, J., May, J., and Wills, J. (2007) 'From coping strategies to tactics: London's low-pay economy and migrant labour', *British Journal of Industrial Relations*, 45(2): 404–432.

[5] Fieldnotes 28 February 2024.

[6] Fieldnotes 7 February 2024, 28 February 2024.

[7] Fieldnotes 25 January 2024.

[8] Fieldnotes 24 April 2024, 3 July 2024.

[9] Fieldnotes 13 March 2024, interviews GA-15, GA-21.

[10] Fieldnotes 14 February 2024.

[11] Boewe, J. and Schulten, J. (2020) 'Amazon strikes in Europe: seven years of industrial action, challenges, and strategies', in J. Alimahomed-Wilson and E. Reese (eds) *The Cost of Free Shipping: Amazon in the Global Economy*, London: Pluto Press, pp 209–224.

[12] Fieldnotes 9 January 2024, 16 January 2024, 13 March 2024.

[13] Fieldnotes 27 March 2024.

[14] Fieldnotes 24 July 2024.

[15] Fieldnotes 3 July 2024.

[16] Fieldnotes 17 September 2024.

[17] Delfanti, A. (2021) *The Warehouse: Workers and Robots at Amazon*, London: Pluto Press, p 146.

[18] Fieldnotes 17 September 2024.

[19] Bernard, D. (2024) 'Amazon faces union-busting legal challenge for QR code ploy', *HR Magazine*, [online] 18 July, Available from: https://www.hrmagazine.co.uk/content/news/amazon-faces-union-busting-legal-challenge-for-qr-code-ploy/ [Accessed 8 November 2024].

[20] Fieldnotes 17 September 2024.

[21] Interview GA-06.

[22] Ibid.

[23] Holgate, J. (2021b) 'Trade unions in the community: building broad spaces of solidarity', *Economic and Industrial Democracy*, 42(2): 226–247.

Reflections on the Fight for Statutory Union Recognition at BHX4

Stuart Richards, GMB Senior Organizer

For union organizers, trade union recognition tends to be seen as an end goal. There's no doubt that it is incredibly important, but, like many of our preconceptions around organizing, our experiences in Amazon challenged the concept of recognition being a final destination. As we saw with the Amazon Labor Union at Staten Island in the US, even when a campaign for recognition is successful, a company that holds an ideological opposition to trade unions will still fervently resist collective bargaining. This shaped how we approached the bids for statutory recognition at Amazon Coventry.

The fundamental aim was to support workers in building their union in their workplace. Ultimately, it is collective, industrial strength that leads to real benefits for workers:

- We supported workers in campaigning for decent pay.
- We built strength through industrial action.
- We helped a network of organic workplace leaders create an effective union structure.
- Amazon Coventry wasn't a union-recognized workplace, but we operated as if it was.

The strategy worked. By 25 April 2023, there were 718 union members at the BHX4 site, just over half the 1,400 employees the company was reporting in December 2022. It looked like we met both tests for statutory recognition – at least 10 per cent of the workers in the proposed bargaining unit in the union and the majority of workers appeared likely to favour recognition. On that basis, we made the first application for recognition. Amazon responded with massive recruitment, increasing the size of the workforce by 93 per cent in 27 days, purely to dilute the number of workers asking for recognition.

We had done wonders for job creation in Coventry, but we were no longer going to meet the tests for statutory recognition. We had little choice but to withdraw the application.

As the union inside BHX4 continued to grow, we started to prepare for the next stage. We were informed both by the experiences of workers in Coventry and colleagues in the global networks we helped to create. The experiences of the Retail, Wholesale and Department Store Union (RWDSU) and their battle for union recognition at Amazon's Bessemer site in the United States were especially relevant.

We knew that the company would invest significant time and resources to stop workers organizing. We knew that the financial cost of this was unlikely to be a factor for Amazon. We also knew that the company would seek to exploit the major weaknesses in the statutory recognition process. Yet the lengths that Amazon bosses would go to still had the capacity to shock us.

An application for statutory recognition was sent to the CAC on 4 March 2024. The documents GMB submitted were full of the stories of Amazon workers and their experiences of the company's union busting. The stories were supplemented by the testimony of GMB at a parliamentary select committee hearing. We were setting the stage for a public battle.

Despite continuing recruitment by Amazon to enlarge the workforce and dilute the percentage of union membership, the CAC took the view that, with a current membership density of 35.62 per cent and taking all other available information about the company into account, they considered it likely that actual support for the GMB was likely to exceed 50 per cent. Consequently, they authorized a ballot. We saw this as an acknowledgement of the huge challenges workers were facing.

The CAC process allows for the union to engage with workers during an 'access period' prior to the ballot, including an opportunity to talk to workers during their working time. We approached Amazon management to put together an access agreement. This is normally fairly straightforward, as it should simply require a schedule of when and where.

Amazon management refused to discuss access directly, insisting that all discussions would need to be undertaken through their legal representatives. We spent the next 52 days bouncing emails between legal teams until we ended with a 17-page *War and Peace* version of an access agreement.

By this point, Amazon workers had experienced 105 days of management's unrelenting union-busting campaign [as outlined in Chapter 4]. The anti-union messaging played to workers' insecurities and created a climate of fear and uncertainty about what recognition might mean. Rumours were spread about union recognition leading to the closure of the site, the removal of benefits, no overtime and no pay awards.

The CAC panel has no official decision-making or mediation powers when it comes to access and cannot force an access agreement on the parties. Even though the agreement placed significant restrictions on the union, including around the ability of workplace leaders to communicate with their colleagues, we had little alternative but to accept the agreement or risk moving forward without agreed access in place.

Amazon's messaging through this period was designed to portray the union as an external organization, a 'business' that could impact negatively on workers' ability to continue earning enough money to live on. We'd seen this in other campaigns in Amazon and we knew it had an impact. Our workplace leaders led the fightback. They were challenging the anti-union rumours on the virtual message board. They were in work and proudly wearing their union t-shirts and hi-vis vests. They were outside talking to workers during shift change. They translated our messaging, and it was their voices that shared it through all of our comms. Despite the huge challenges and intimidation, they held the line that the workers were the union, and they were already inside.

As we entered the access period, a small part of BHX4 became the Workers' Republic of Amazon. For four weeks, three display screens and a notice board proudly shone with the faces of union members and their messages about what union recognition would mean for workers. For two weeks, workplace leaders joined union organizers in speaking to around 2,000 workers inside the workplace. The message from our leaders was simple: 'We know what it's like to work without union recognition. We've seen the benefits we've lost. We've had to deal with the issues that management refuse to address. We now get to make a decision based on who we trust to look after our interests – the workers who've built our union, or the bosses that are spending massive amounts of money telling us to vote no.' Not surprisingly, this remained the one message that Amazon management avoided trying to tackle.

Outside of our small part of BHX4, the rest of the site remained drenched in anti-union propaganda. This continued after our window of workplace meetings and into the final ballot period. Amazon was also able to send anti-union material through the company mobile phone app that workers have to use for details of work. GMB had no access to this. Amazon were able to send managers to put pressure on workers through direct anti-union conversations on the shop floor.

The massive disparity in access and the overwhelming union-busting had an undeniable impact.

The results of the ballot were confirmed on 17 July. It stated that there were 3,012 workers in the proposed bargaining unit: 2,601 workers voted in the ballot (86 per cent of the total bargaining unit), 1,281 workers voted for union recognition (49.5 per cent of the valid vote) and 1,309 workers did not vote for union recognition (50.5 per cent of the valid vote).

There are still unanswered questions hanging around. For instance, the 11 ballot papers deemed as 'spoiled or otherwise invalid' or what actions were taken with the list of 44 workers who confirmed that they would not be at work during the workplace ballot, which was sent to both the CAC and Amazon. But the reality remains that the vote was lost by 29 votes.

We all felt devastated and there were plenty of tears, but we were back on the gate on the day of the results. We were there with the words of Darren, one of our original workplace leaders, ringing in our ears:

> I have seen total strangers become a family, I have seen
> a real unity among people from every race, religion

and country come together. Amazon spent millions on stopping us. We gave our free time, we asked people across Coventry to volunteer to help us, and what did we achieve. The world looked at us and showed their support. We pushed a multi trillion company to fight dirty and we bloodied their nose.

At the start of the latest bid for union recognition at Amazon Coventry, we talked about using the process to highlight and challenge the huge issues with the statutory recognition process. Our case study has now been presented to the new Labour government. Amazon workers took their story to Parliament and talked about the change we need to see. Out of our ten asks in the case study, eight have made it into the first reading of the Employment Rights Bill. Legislation to change the CAC process and support workers in organizing their workplace is being shaped by the voices and experiences of the union members in Amazon Coventry.

Right back at the start, we also talked about the likelihood that we would need to make multiple applications for recognition before we won. We're not going away, the union inside Amazon warehouses continues to grow and union recognition is just a ballot away.

5

Developing Leadership

The importance of building leadership among workers is expressed by the GMB organizing principle that: 'People are strongest when they organise themselves'.[1] As Gall and Fiorito argue, leadership by lay members within the workplace is critical for both recruitment of new members and translating members' commitment to the union into active participation.[2] Recognizing organic, or natural, leaders among the workforce and integrating them into trade union structures is central to McAlevey's approach to organizing,[3] and was a major goal for GMB organizers at BHX4.

As well as the benefits for democratic inclusion and effective organizing, building worker leadership also had important practical implications for the GMB's capacity to extend their success at BHX4 to other sites. Unionizing one site, BHX4, required a considerable concentration of the region's resources in terms of organizers' time as well as funds. Replicating this at other sites would therefore only be possible to the extent that GMB workers at BHX4 took leadership and reduced the need for involvement of paid organizers. Developing leadership at BHX4 could also greatly accelerate unionization of other Amazon sites, through the involvement of BHX4 worker-leaders speaking to workers at the gates, with the moral authority and shared understanding that they carried as fellow Amazon workers. Whether by freeing up organizers' time at BHX4 or travelling to other warehouses themselves, developing worker leadership was therefore critical to extending the space of organizing to other warehouses. This chapter discusses the challenges involved in developing leadership at BHX4 and how the GMB responded.

Challenges in developing leadership

This section presents the primary challenges in developing a leadership at BHX4 that could effectively represent the diverse and divided workforce described in Chapters 3 and 4. These challenges were particularly acute because of Amazon's recruitment and promotion practices, which worker-leaders described as promoting divisions along national lines. This can be seen to some extent as a local reflection of the spatial structuring of global capitalism by nation states,[4] but was intensified and even weaponized by Amazon's own practices.

Feliz Leon reports that in the early stages of the union drive in 2022, the BHX4 workforce was around 70 per cent African (mostly from East Africa), 20 per cent Eastern European and the remaining 10 per cent a mix of South Asian, English, Anglophone Caribbean and Brazilian workers.[5] As GMB membership grew and worker-leaders emerged within these communities, Amazon notably increased its recruitment of South Asian workers, including many international students who were outside the GMB's established networks, as worker-leaders consistently described:

> Going just one side of the continent, recruiting massively, and giving them the opportunity to work together ... With that number, they can make everything difficult if they really don't want to support the GMB ... I'm talking about the massive India recruitment. Because as it is today, I think 70, 80 per cent of the people working in BHX4 is Indians. (Global Majority worker-leader GA-05)

Another worker-leader highlighted the susceptibility to Amazon's arguments that arose from these new workers' lack of experience with the company:

> [T]emporary contract ... most of them are Indian students ... some of them, they came only a year before ... So, they don't know about the UK ... So, they try to believe Amazon. So ... that's ... [why] Amazon find that easier to brainwash these people, instead of brainwash the people who was working [at Amazon] for six years. (Global Majority worker-leader GA-32)

In addition, many worker-leaders reported promotion practices that gave preference to a managers' 'circle' of favoured workers, often from the same country of origin. This was reportedly enabled by Amazon policies that gave line managers discretion over which workers had the opportunity to gain 'step up' management experience, an essential criterion for internal promotion.[6] The following account is typical of many reports by worker-leaders, with a consistent picture painted by worker-leaders of different ethnicities:

> They are Asian from same, his [manager's] community. So, he did racist with me because I'm from Pakistan. He's from India and he did racial behaviour with me. He took his people who … are only two months in Amazon, he give them a Lead position … He took only from his community, from his background. (Global Majority worker-leader GA-15)

It was also suggested by some worker-leaders that if a worker raised a complaint against a manager, this would invariably be handled by another member of the same circle.[7] Another worker-leader described how these circles had operated in their experience to both block their progression and then to victimize them for raising concerns:

> Alongside fellow Associates, I sought training for a specific role to enable fair rotation, but a supervisor showed clear favouritism, allowing only those of his background into this perceived 'desirable' role. This led to a hostile work environment fuelled by intimidation, bullying, and racism. Despite many Associates lodging grievances over the years, formal hearings were persistently dismissed. When I raised it formally, I faced extreme retaliation, was pushed out of my department as they claimed it was 'under investigation', and endured financial hardship and mental health challenges … This culture of favouritism and retaliation continued, affecting promotions as well. Though I passed the interview for a leadership position, I was misled about an opening, only to see a position awarded to someone

who had contributed to the hostile environment
I reported. (Global Majority worker-leader GA-16)

These circles were described as often operating along national and
ethnic lines, promoting divisions, competition and resentment among
workers that made it harder to build a coordinated leadership. This
represents a contemporary remaking of longstanding practices of
racial capitalism,[8] and stands in stark contradiction to Amazon's
professed commitment to equality.[9]

The GMB's response to developing leadership

This section examines how GMB organizers supported the
development of worker-leaders at BHX4, beginning with the
internal arrangements of the organizing team and moving on to
explore the use of strike time, member surveys and a leadership
training programme. The results of this leadership development
are then considered, including worker-leaders' evolving
relationship to the rest of the union, their ability to articulate
collective injuries and victories, and their political understanding
of the struggle at BHX4.

Developing an effective leadership among workers organized
through the GMB required a strong relationship between worker-
leaders and organizers. Adding to the risk that the union would be
seen as a third-party body external to workers, which was an idea
actively promoted by Amazon,[10] the vast majority of organizers
were not from the same communities as workers, being mostly
white British. However, they were deeply embedded in experiences
of work, in many cases having backgrounds in other low-paid
occupations where they first trained and worked as volunteer reps
before later moving into paid employment with the union, as this
organizer described:

> I was new as an organizer, but not new in experiences
> in organizing, because … I'd worked in hand with the
> organizing team. So, I'd spent years building my skills as
> an organizer and learning those skills [as a rep in another
> sector]. I'd come off the apprenticeship training and all of
> that … was about building structures, looking for organic

leaders, listening to our members and letting them lead the way. (European organizer GA-08)

This expresses the systematic embedding of a worker-led approach within the region, both through the recruitment of worker-leaders as organizers and through the content of their training. This resonates with the concept in organizational psychology of 'servant leadership', which Kaminski finds to be particularly relevant and effective for trade unions. The servant leader 'helps the followers develop their skills and reach their goals ... [and] puts the followers' needs before their own personal gain'.[11] This expresses the relationship of leading organizers to worker-leaders at BHX4, and the relationship of organizers and worker-leaders to the wider membership and workforce.

These characteristics of the organizer team were accompanied by operational flexibility. Two regional organizing teams were brought together in the BHX4 campaign, and an experienced Regional Education Officer was allocated the task of supporting the development of worker-leaders. An organizer described the combination of collective working, delegation and mentoring in the BHX4 campaign:

> [T]hat's the big difference between Rugeley and Coventry ... A lot more shared leadership. Historically in the union, you would be one organizer, one sheet, one responsibility. Where we work in the organizing team [on BHX4], so it's not just my project ... everybody's pulling their own thing and doing their own piece, we're all working together as a team. (European organizer GA-08)

As part of this approach, newer organizers described how they were given considerable freedom to take responsibility for defined areas of work and try out new methods.

In seeking to identify and develop leadership, organizers described strikes as creating a productive time and space. Picket lines were used by organizers to identify organic leaders among the GMB membership by observing interactions, as an organizer described:

> Whenever there's a strike ... we are constantly looking for ... natural leaders ... organic leaders ... who's the

person that's telling people what to do, who's the person that people are going to and asking what to do or are gathered around ... so even now some of our newer key players have been picked off the picket lines from the organizers looking and taking that time ... Our job is a lot of looking and listening to [see] what's actually happening on that picket line to find those key people. (European organizer GA-08)

Another organizer described the use of strike days to test workers' willingness to take on more responsibility with the union by asking them to carry out tasks with other members:

You always see a cluster of [people] ... and you always find the leader of that. And ... to get more proactively involved and then start getting them to pass the messages ... to see, are they actually leaders, by saying: 'Brother, I've got a job for you, I really need your help. Can you do X, Y, and Z for me on the picket line?' And when they're doing it, you're like, yep, he's definitely, or she is definitely on it. You get the details and you build the relationship before you even invite them to the meeting ... 'Cause some people are fantastic at being leaders, but they don't want to be [a] proactive leader. And that's where we've ... found those leaders. (Global Majority organizer GA-14)

This systematic approach to identifying leaders through the constructed space of the picket line was combined with gathering information about the networks and relationships operating inside the warehouse. During some of the early strikes at BHX4, 'strike schools' were held, mapping out the different departments and shifts across the warehouse to identify where worker-leaders had contacts and influence, and where there were gaps. This is an important part of McAlevey's method and has a longer history in the GMB that an experienced organizer dated back to the TUC Organizing Academy in the early 2000s.[12] An organizer explained:

[W]e've had to be creative with the time that we've got ... using the dispute and the strike time ... because every other time people [are] at work or with family. Most people are working 60 hours a week ... And then some of them ... [have] second jobs ... So those first strikes that we had ... we would run strike schools and it would be everything from mapping the workplace, literally pulling up big sheets of paper and drawing that workplace out and looking at all the different departments and then them saying, 'I work here', and, 'I work there' ... and, 'I know someone that works there and works there' ... And ... we're still doing that now. (European organizer GA-08)

The autonomous space of the strike schools during strike time, initiated by the organizers but co-produced with worker-leaders, thereby generated knowledge about the spatial, temporal and social layout of the warehouse that enabled worker-leaders to strategically extend their reach. These strike schools were also used as democratic fora to plan future strike dates and shape all of the messaging that the organizers used in printed and digital communications to members, including writing scripts for videos, which were then produced with the assistance of organizers. Mapping was maintained and continually updated through discussion with worker-leaders, assisted by phone banking prior to every strike ballot.

In developing this leadership strategically, GMB organizers recognized the importance of different communities of workers based around nationality and the significance of this for organic leadership. This is part of a growing recognition among trade unions of the importance of worker identities as an axis of oppression and mobilization.[13] At the same time, GMB organizers aimed to work beyond these national groupings to build a united leadership in which different communities were represented, but understood themselves as part of a shared struggle. Although the leaders of the initial wildcat walkouts came from many different nationalities, the first generation of worker-leaders who had most contact with GMB organizers were not representative of the full range of nationalities and languages among the membership, the majority being white and British. This gradually changed, as organizers and worker-leaders built up relationships of trust with a wider range of workers, among whom new worker-leaders emerged. In the autumn of 2023, organizers conducted an online survey where they invited all members to nominate who they saw as leaders in their part of the warehouse. An organizer described:

> [W]e sent out a survey ... where we asked people to nominate somebody within their section or department or shift. And it was really the kind of questions of 'Who does everybody look up to?', 'Who's the person that's happy to help others?', 'Who's the person that's happy to stand up for others?', 'Who's the person that will help you sort your problems out?', 'Who's the person that will listen to others?' ... Those are the kind of questions that we asked people to think about and ... then we took that nomination list, and we had about 60-something people nominated and some of them [were] nominated multiple times. (Global Majority organizer GA-14)

Organizers worked with the list of nominated workers, having one-to-one conversations and eventually producing a working list for a 'leadership group', which continued to be added to as new leaders emerged on the picket line.[14] It was evident from comments by many of the worker-leaders identified through this process that they took pride in working hard in their job and felt respected by other workers for this,[15] consistent with a common pattern observed by McAlevey.[16] None reported any prior experience of trade union leadership, and most had little experience of any kind with trade unions prior to joining the GMB at Amazon.

This leadership group were invited to weekly day-long meetings, beginning in January 2024, for which they took unpaid leave from Amazon and were reimbursed by the GMB for loss of earnings and expenses. These meetings combined elements of the GMB's reps training in order to enable worker-leaders to represent other members at work, and democratic discussions involving worker-leaders and organizers, which shaped the union's strategy at every step. Regular votes were called to make key decisions, as part of an experiential education in union democracy. Participants reflected positively on these sessions:

> I enjoy these training days. I enjoy listening. He [the organizer leading the sessions] knows how to encourage

us ... [H]e doesn't give us bullshit, you know. If it's wrong, wrong, he will say it right away. If it's good, good, he will say it ... And he's ready to listen ... I'm learning a lot, actually. And ... whatever you need ... you tell them [the organizers] and they ... will try to support you. (Global Majority worker-leader GA-01)

Initially it was envisaged by organizers that this leadership programme would comprise six or seven sessions,[17] but due to the constantly evolving situation at BHX4 and the emergence of new leaders, meetings continued and were still running as of September 2024. This autonomous democratic space was crucial to enable the worker-leaders to be part of directing the campaign.

On some occasions, these 'leader days' included parallel sessions, where some organizers trained new reps while longstanding worker-leaders worked on different tasks involved in running the campaign, and the whole group came together to make strategic decisions. This process was facilitated by organizers, who centred workers' own experiences, consistent with McAlevey's ethos of Freirean education, and reflected back by posing questions that led workers to discover new things for themselves. This mirrored the benefits for workers' empowerment that Smith also identifies in educational practices by newer 'indie' unions, when members' own experiences are incorporated within union learning.[18] At times, GMB organizers would make interventions to prompt worker-leaders to reflect on how they could use other workers' experiences to build resistance. For example, in one session, an organizer argued that: 'Anger moves people, but what moves them even more is hope. We need to find ways of talking to people in a way that turns that justifiable anger into hope.'[19] Each worker-leader was also assigned an organizer as a mentor, with contact expected at least every couple of days.[20]

In these meetings, organizers did not passively follow members' lead, but actively contributed to rigorous discussion. This was evident, for example, in a meeting between organizers and 13 worker-leaders that decided the union's strategy for the recognition ballot.[21] A discussion on whether to hold this ballot by post or within the workplace was introduced by an organizer who outlined a set of pros and cons for each option, but proposed that on balance, a postal ballot would be preferable. After an initial discussion, the organizer called for an indicative vote by the worker-leaders that came out 12 to 1 in favour of a workplace ballot. Because this was not unanimous, the organizer opened up the discussion again, with important interventions being made by worker-leaders describing the difficulty many workers faced in terms of receiving post in shared accommodation, and organizers sharing information about the regulations covering the ballot process. After a lengthy and vigorous discussion, another vote was taken, this time expressing unanimous support for a workplace ballot. In this way, organizers provided legal and political expertise and facilitated a democratic process in which worker-leaders developed their collective ability to make informed judgements, which in this case was the reverse of that initially favoured by organizers.

Between January and April 2024, the leadership group grew dramatically in confidence and became much more representative of the wider workforce. The union produced GMB t-shirts for worker-leaders to wear within the workplace, whose design and slogans were decided in the weekly leader meetings, to increase their visibility and encourage other workers to approach them with concerns. Many worker-leaders spoke about how their involvement in the leadership group had developed skills and confidence and changed their relationship with other workers. In some cases this involved the self-discovery of qualities and capabilities of which they were previously unaware – for example:

> I can probably say that in ... 25 minutes, I can convince anybody to join the union ... [Before] I didn't recognize myself as well as a leadership and ... ability to talk ... [to] a hundred, thousand people in front of the strike. [Now] I can talk easily. I can convince them. So, this learning's come from ... join the unions. (Global Majority worker-leader GA-15)

Another worker-leader described the ramifications of the growing visibility and confidence of this leadership within the workplace:

> [Y]ou can just feel it's a better atmosphere among the people. People are talking more ... It's great to see people, not so much enjoying their work, but being happy to

be in that community that the union brought into the workplace ... There's a few people that I've got to represent over the next few weeks ... [and] before ... they would never speak to me ... with different communities and different lifestyles. But they're my best mates now. They'll come and speak to me, and they'll be like 'Oh, [name], I need to mention this' ... I'll be like 'OK, don't worry' ... So, representing people ... has really helped push it forward. (European worker-leader GA-02)

Some also emphasized the depth of trust that was made possible by recruiting leaders 'from the inside', among the workforce:

I look at my colleagues now and ... they look at me and they trust me because they know me ... What the most successful for us was, was ... they [GMB organizers] create leaders for us ... And the union, they create this representative ... from the inside ... they create and recruit people ... from us. From ... my colleague. And ... now ... we trust more ... in [the] union ... all the time they said to us: 'You are the union' ... this message was very important. (European migrant worker-leader GA-21)

The consistent reminder referenced here, that workers 'are the union', exemplifies the empowering language advocated by McAlevey and expanded on by Allinson.[22]

The importance of this leadership group, and its growing confidence, was evident in worker-leaders' evolving relationship with the wider union. For example, in April 2024, a group of worker-leaders, most from Global Majority migrant backgrounds, gave an extremely confident presentation to the GMB Midlands Regional Council, with one Global Majority leader telling the meeting: 'What we have achieved is not a list of accomplishments, it's a transformation.'[23] Another Global Majority leader at this meeting used the metaphor of a bundle of sticks that can be broken individually but become stronger together as an example of how he explained the union to his colleagues. A white British worker-leader explained how representing other workers had given him a greater understanding of the challenges faced by East African workers after seeing them targeted repeatedly by managers. Illustrating what he had learned through this experience, he criticized Amazon for making no allowances for circumstances that might require an East African worker to take time off work, for example, to visit a sick family member in a war zone, and who then might encounter problems trying to get back to the UK by a designated date, but lack internet access to inform their employer immediately.[24] Further reinforcing the development of this leadership, my fieldnotes from July 2024 recorded:

> The level of confidence and comfort of the workers with each other, with organisers and being in the GMB regional [office] … and their level of contact with workers across shifts and departments, have all come a long way since the first leaders training sessions in January.[25]

By July 2024, 15 BHX4 workers had been formally trained and designated as GMB reps, a further 30 were considered active members of a Communication Action Network to coordinate between different departments and shifts, and some worker-leaders were being paid by the union to represent members at other Amazon warehouses across the region and to identify organic leaders within those sites.[26]

Organizers' commitment to involve workers in every important decision brought their expert knowledge of the workplace and workforce cultures within the organizing process, capitalizing on the power of workers' knowledge that Kassem highlights.[27] It was only possible to engage the workers in this democratic process by creating spaces and times beyond Amazon's control, including the strike day pickets, meetings and strike schools, and the weekly leaders' meetings, all enabled by union payments to cover lost income. The creation of these autonomous spaces was particularly important because of Amazon's systematic use of 'internal marketing' to gain consent from its employees,[28] demonstrated most powerfully at BHX4 through the company's monopoly control of the space of the warehouse and workers' time to pursue ideological hegemony in the period leading to the recognition ballot, which was discussed further in Chapter 4.

While GMB organizers placed central importance on worker-leaders taking ownership of the campaign, it was also clearly evident that these leaders greatly valued the support they received from the wider union and its paid organizers. Illustrating this, a worker-leader argued: 'I cannot, just by me ... help these people. I need guidance... So, I think this is a ... big, big union. This union can help us, can show us the way ... really ... how to handle this thing' (Global Majority worker-leader GA-01).

This is vital when we consider the findings of Boewe and Schulten that the strength of the Ver.di union in German Amazon warehouses was rooted in 'shop-floor activists', but that they 'tend to be overburdened' and require from the union 'more assistance to adequately support the activists under pressure'.[29] In the case of BHX4, at certain key points, such as the meetings that the union was allowed to hold within the workplace during the CAC-regulated 'access period' prior to the recognition ballot, worker-leaders made it clear to organizers that the wider membership needed the reassurance of direct input from paid GMB organizers in those meetings, and that in some ways the workers had more confidence in the organizers than in the worker-leaders.[30] A worker-leader expressed this as follows:

> They [the organizers] show us they're strong. They show us that somebody's behind us ... if we have a meeting with [workers] ... [the organizers] have to show up to talk ... not just ... my colleague [worker-leaders]. For instance, if you go in a meeting and you have a serious problem, and if you go with just your colleague, not with your representative ... people don't trust you. They say: 'Look, I pay for what [through GMB membership]?' (European migrant worker-leader GA-21)

It is worth bearing findings from other union contexts in mind here, such as Sadler's study of an education union in the US, which found that members' participation was influenced more by their perceptions of higher-level paid union leaders than workplace leaders.[31] This is a complex issue, which can be understood as connected to the level of confidence workers have in themselves and in people they see as similar to them. It is also perhaps connected for some with perceptions of the GMB as a professional service provider, as opposed to the GMB's intention to be a self-organized workers collective. Yet, reliance on paid organizers was also as a means of accessing the depth of support from the union. It became clear, particularly during Amazon's aggressive anti-union campaign in the period leading up to the recognition ballot, that worker-leaders were under intense pressure; in this context, involvement from organizers gave reassurance because they operated outside the space controlled by Amazon. While organizers were also under great pressure, and in the period leading up to the recognition ballot reported disrupted sleep, colds, rashes and exhaustion,[32] their greater distance from the workplace and freedom from the threat of disciplinary action by Amazon enabled them to provide important external support to worker-leaders, with frequent reassurance that if worker-leaders were victimized by Amazon for their union activity, then organizers would support them.[33] A similar picture has been found elsewhere – for example, Holgate reports precarious workers outside of regular employment and organized through Unite the Union's Community wing saying that they valued membership of Unite for having a large organization behind them and saw no contradiction between this and their grassroots activism.[34]

Support provided to worker-leaders by organizers in the weekly leaders' meetings and through one-to-one mentoring and informal conversations was supplemented by direct lines of communication between organizers and the wider membership, which included: meetings inside Amazon during the access period; WhatsApp groups where members could ask questions; an online 'truth kit' that aimed to challenge Amazon's claims about unions and dispel common misconceptions; and a series of mass meetings on two strike days in May and June 2024, where worker-leaders and organizers spoke with up to 300 workers at a time. As well as group discussions on WhatsApp, organizers described how they would often respond to questions members had raised on these groups by phoning that individual for a longer discussion.[35]

Adding to this wider support for worker-leaders, organizers arranged and shared with workers video messages of support from parliamentarians and media reports, and a public petition that had received 13,000 signatories by the time the recognition ballot opened.[36] The election of a Labour government just prior to the recognition ballot, whose leader Keir Starmer had publicly supported the call for recognition at BHX4, provided a notable boost to worker-leaders' morale. All of this emphasizes the importance of a wider union structure, and other support received through campaigning, to bolster worker-leaders' confidence against employer opposition within a tightly controlled workplace, as will be discussed further in Chapter 7.

An important consequence of this leadership was the development of narratives identifying injustices that were widely and deeply felt across the workforce, informed by worker-leaders' contact with other workers and their growing knowledge of workers' rights gained through the leadership programme. For example, one discussion between worker-leaders and organizers identified: a lack of reasonable adjustments for workers' disabilities and health conditions; unfair ADAPTs for idle time; unclean toilets; lack of overtime opportunities; 'letters of concern' (a precursor to disciplinary measures) being issued in response to time off for illness; various safety issues and safety boots that hurt workers' feet; reduced size of lockers that meant workers couldn't leave work clothes on site; poor-quality and small portions of food and a lack of certified halal options; unfair shift rotations and favouritism; and a 'contemplation room' for prayer that was unfit for purpose and had broken washing facilities for the previous six weeks.[37] Such direct insights from worker-leaders were combined with a survey conducted by GMB organizers at that time that received 1,000 responses, of which 300 complained of the lack of certified halal food, 350 complained of dirt and 250 complained of uncomfortable temperatures. The discussion of these combined sources of information from worker-leaders and organizers led to a petition circulated by worker-leaders concerning Associates' experience with their safety boots, with a view to using this to launch a collective grievance.[38]

In some cases, injustices were not simply described but also situated by worker-leaders within an analysis of political economy. For example, at one meeting, a worker-leader presented a calculation that, on average, Amazon makes a profit of £1.75 per item, and used this to calculate the degree of exploitation of workers processing these items.[39] Often, such an analysis was situated in a wider socioeconomic context, and emerged in tandem with a growing experience of collective action that encouraged personal problems to be understood socially, as this worker-leader described:

Because we were all suffering. Obviously, the gas, electric [prices] had gone [up], the petrol was going through the roof as well … It was everything. And … I personally felt alone. I thought it was just me that was struggling … to pay bills … But then when you're in a crowd and everyone's beating the same drum, it's [a feeling], 'I'm not alone in this' … Amazon, the richest company in the world, was paying us, I think it was, eight pence above minimum wage, after all the stuff we did [for the company]. (European worker-leader GA-02)

Some leaders situated their struggle in other ways, extending solidarity across generations and countries, as the following passage from my strike fieldnotes recorded:

[An African worker-leader] spoke on [the] sound system, demanded Amazon treat us like humans and appealed to other workers to keep up the fight, if not for themselves then for those coming after them – cousins, nephews, aunties, who may have only just arrived in the country – we need to fight now so they will be treated better. Then spoke on Palestine as another front in the same struggle, led chants of 'Free Palestine'.[40]

Such expansive connections between issues that may appear on the surface to be unconnected are consistent with longstanding traditions of anti-imperialist humanism, as articulated, for example, by Guinean theorist and leader Amilcar Cabral, who argues that a struggle in one time and place can be seen as one of many fronts in an international struggle against capitalism and imperialism.[41] This can be seen as cultivating among worker-leaders what Boyle describes as 'discursive power', a critical resource for union revitalization and the building of wider support for workers' struggles.[42]

The greatest test of the leaders' group came with their narrow defeat in the recognition ballot in 2024. Worker-leaders and organizers reflected on the implications of this defeat and discussed their next steps across a series of meetings, showing the kind of open discussion and honesty about setbacks advocated by McAlevey and Allinson.[43] Over the course of these discussions, a co-produced strategy evolved that aimed to challenge Amazon to live up to the promises it had made in its campaign against recognition, while deepening and broadening the GMB's activity across other Amazon UK sites in preparation for the next round of struggle. One of these meetings was addressed in person by the General Secretary of the GMB, emphasizing support for the BHX4 workers at the highest levels of the union.

Overall, the development of worker-leaders at BHX4 required the creation of autonomous spaces and times through strike pickets, mass meetings and leaders' days. This built the confidence, moral authority and skills of worker-leaders to challenge Amazon's hegemony over the time and space of the warehouse, and to name and call out its harmful effects. The wider union structure, extending far outside Amazon's control, provided a depth of support for worker-leaders that enabled them to sustain their advocacy of workers' independent interests even in the face of intense opposition from Amazon and despite the power that Amazon held over them because of their reliance on its wages.

These issues have wider relevance because of the importance of working-class leadership for democracy and for effective resistance to capitalist exploitation. The relative weakness of working-class movements in Britain in recent decades, when considered from a historical and international perspective, and the limited reach of Britain's traditional trade unions, particularly among poorer and more diverse sections of the working class,[44] mean that the development of leaders among these sections of society must often rely on people with little or no prior experience. Yet, as the working class becomes increasingly diverse[45] and increasingly precarious,[46] the development of such leaders becomes increasingly important for the working class as a whole. The GMB's experience at BHX4 provides important lessons in how this can be addressed.

Reflective questions for organizers, worker-leaders and activists

- What were the main challenges for the GMB building worker leadership at BHX4?
- How were these challenges addressed?

- What challenges do you face building worker leadership in your organizing?
- How do you address these and how could you further improve?

Notes

1   GMB (2024) 'Make Work Better: GMB workplace representatives and shop stewards induction course, part 1 (Autumn 2024–Summer 2025 ed.)'.
2   Gall, G. and Fiorito, J. (2012) 'Toward better theory on the relationship between commitment, participation and leadership in unions', *Leadership & Organization Development Journal*, 33(8): 715–731.
3   McAlevey, J.F. (2016) *No Shortcuts: Organizing for Power*, Oxford: Oxford University Press; McAlevey, J.F. (2023) *Rules to Win By: Power and Participation in Union Negotiations*, Oxford: Oxford University Press.
4   Mezzadra, S. and Neilson, B. (2013) *Border as Method, or, the Multiplication of Labour*, Durham, NC: Duke University Press; Vickers, T. (2019) *Borders, Migration and Class: Producing Immigrants and Workers*, Bristol: Bristol University Press.
5   Feliz Leon, L. (2024) 'Will immigrant workers in Britain win Europe's first Amazon union?', *Labor Notes*, [online] 15 July, Available from: https://labornotes.org/2024/07/will-immigrant-workers-britain-win-UK-first-amazon-union [Accessed 8 November 2024].
6   Fieldnotes 07 February 2024, 24 June 2024.
7   Fieldnotes 31 January 2024, 27 March 2024.
8   Bhattacharyya, G. (2023) *The Futures of Racial Capitalism*, London: Polity.
9   Kassem, S. (2023) *Work and Alienation in the Platform Economy: Amazon and the Power of Organisation*, Bristol: Bristol University Press, p 83.
10 Fieldnotes 24 June 2024.
11 Kaminski, M. (2024) 'Effective union leadership: evidence from the Harvard Trade Union Program', *Labor Studies Journal*, 49(1): 5–27, at 11.
12 Communication with GA-06 16 September 2024; see also Simms, M., Holgate, J. and Heery, E. (2013) *Union Voices: Tactics and Tensions in UK Organizing*, Ithaca, NY: Cornell University Press.
13 Doellgast, V., Bidwell, M. and Colvin, A.J.S. (2021) 'New directions in employment relations theory: understanding fragmentation, identity, and legitimacy', *ILR Review*, 74(3): 555–579.
14 Interview GA-14.
15 Fieldnotes 3 July 2024.
16 McAlevey (2016) (n 3).
17 Fieldnotes 9 January 2024.

[18] Smith, H. (2022) 'The "indie unions" and the UK labour movement: towards a community of practice', *Economic and Industrial Democracy*, 43(3): 1369–1390.

[19] Fieldnotes 24 April 2024.

[20] Fieldnotes 16 January 2024.

[21] Fieldnotes 13 March 2024.

[22] Allinson, I. (2022) *Workers Can Win: A Guide to Organising at Work*, London: Pluto Press, p 75.

[23] Fieldnotes 24 April 2024.

[24] Fieldnotes 24 April 2024.

[25] Fieldnotes 3 July 2024.

[26] Interview with organizer GA-08.

[27] Kassem (n 9), p 80.

[28] Delfanti, A. (2021) *The Warehouse: Workers and Robots at Amazon*, London: Pluto Press, p 83.

[29] Boewe, J. and Schulten, J. (2020) 'Amazon strikes in Europe: seven years of industrial action, challenges, and strategies', in J. Alimahomed-Wilson and E. Reese (eds) *The Cost of Free Shipping: Amazon in the Global Economy*, London: Pluto Press, pp 209–224, at p 221.

[30] Fieldnotes 18 June 2024.

[31] Sadler, J. (2012) 'The importance of multiple leadership roles in fostering participation', *Leadership & Organization Development Journal*, 33(8): 779–796.

[32] Fieldnotes 18 June 2024.

[33] Fieldnotes 24 April 2024.

[34] Holgate, J. (2021) 'Trade unions in the community: building broad spaces of solidarity', *Economic and Industrial Democracy*, 42(2): 226–247.

[35] Fieldnotes 28 February 2024.

[36] Fieldnotes 18 June 2024.

[37] Fieldnotes 28 February 2024.

[38] Fieldnotes 28 February 2024.

[39] Fieldnotes 31 January 2024.

[40] Fieldnotes 20 March 2024.

[41] Cabral, A. (1964) 'Brief analysis of the social structure in Guinea', *Marxist Internet Archive* [online], Available from: https://www.marxists.org/subject/africa/cabral/1964/bassg.htm [Accessed 11 November 2024].

[42] Boyle, K.A. (2024) 'The discursive power of trade union leadership: framing identity fields for public persuasion', *Work, Employment and Society*, DOI:10.1177/09500170241279778.

[43] Allinson (n 22); McAlevey (n 3).

[44] Però, D. (2020) 'Indie unions, organising and labour renewal: learning from precarious migrant workers', *Work, Employment and Society*,

34(5): 900–918; Holgate, J. (2021) *Arise: Power, Strategy and Union Resurgence*, London: Pluto Press.

[45] Catney, G. et al (2023) 'Ethnic diversification and neighbourhood mixing: a rapid response analysis of the 2021 Census of England and Wales', *Geographical Journal*, 189(1): 63–77.

[46] Formby, A., Sheikh, M., and Jeffery, B. (2024) 'The global disappearance of decent work? Precarity, exploitation, and work-based harms in the neoliberal era', *Social Inclusion*, 12: 8755.

ESSAY 6

Representing Members Inside Amazon

Paramanathan Pradeep, GMB worker-leader at BHX4

This is a challenging job because Amazon do the investigation process without GMB reps. Associates are often not well informed about their rights; this can lead them to say things that harm their case. The stakes are high – sometimes the outcome of a disciplinary process can be dismissal. Amazon always prepares a lot of paperwork for each case. As GMB reps, we have to go through all the pages, spending extra hours on this. We need reps from all the departments, sometimes there are health and safety policies for a certain department that Associates and reps from outside that department won't know.

Amazon's 'idle time' system is a source of many complaints. It is often inconsistent and unfair. This could give grounds for a collective grievance against Amazon.

Agitate, Educate, Organize! How We Trained and Developed Workplace Leaders

Tom Rigby, GMB Regional Education Officer

The campaign to unionize BHX4 set challenges that the traditional framework for trade union education is not equipped to address. We had to create space for workers to learn and organize. The traditional framework assumes a legal entitlement to paid release in a workplace where the union is recognized. Without recognition and paid release, two issues arise:

1. How are the workers going to get the free time to undertake training?
2. How are we going to ensure that they are not penalized financially for taking on the role of workplace leader?

We dealt with this by workers taking unpaid leave and paying loss of earnings from union funds. This amounts to a substantial investment by the union, but without it, there would have been no realistic prospect of having the time required to train a group of leaders capable of going head to head with a powerful, well-organized and resourced management in a prolonged struggle.

Underlying the approach we applied at BHX4 is a distinctive philosophy of workers education: the idea that there is no task that workers cannot handle and no problem they cannot solve. This fits with the GMB's longstanding commitment to workers' control and industrial democracy.

Put briefly, workers' education is a joint process where workers become aware of their own collective power. This means that the role of educators/organizers is not to tell workers what to think, but simply to get them to analyse the situation they face and work out strategies to deal with that situation.

Throughout the process of building the collective leadership at BHX4, we spent a significant amount of time getting the messaging right. This is the process of talking through how to hold organizing conversations with workers. An organizing conversation has three elements.

- Agitate: get the worker to talk about and identify the unfairness of a situation.
- Educate: help the worker identify why this injustice is happening and see how we have the power to challenge it.
- Organize: identify with the worker a collective action they can take to challenge the employer.

The workers would look at what people were saying on the shop floor and then think through how to respond. Different approaches would be tried and tested out. One fantastic example of this was the main video for the recognition ballot. The script was taken from the words and phrases the workers themselves developed.

In the Amazon campaign, the GMB staff running the training sessions were functioning as educator/organizers. It was not simply a process of imparting knowledge and checking it had been understood; the entire training programme was based around workers themselves identifying problems, developing solutions and applying them.

There is, of course, a role for imparting knowledge, whether that be about health and safety legislation, recognition law, disciplinary procedures or the history of the working-class movement, but that role is subordinate to and governed by the need to help the workers learn how to organize themselves.

The role of the educator/organizer is not just to facilitate discussion and draw ideas out; there must also be a degree of challenge. If the workers are looking at a particular initiative, it is beholden on the educator/organizer to ensure that the pros and cons are discussed properly and thought through. This doesn't necessarily mean that the union officer gets the reps to abandon a course of action; it can quite often mean the exact opposite. A good example of this at BHX4 would be the discussions around having a workplace or postal ballot for recognition. The initial steer from organizers was towards a postal ballot, but it was the workplace leaders who in a process of thinking through the options came up with the workplace ballot as the preferred option.

A central aim for organizers at BHX4 was to help workers take control and lead. Many of the training sessions involved a discussion about some immediate tactical issue that we needed to decide. Whenever this happened and options were developed, it was vital to have a vote among the workplace leaders. Workers get to decide very little in their working lives, so having a vote in the union really matters. It is vital to getting workers to see themselves as the union and not the union as a third party made up of full-time staff. By taking votes, they are asserting their authority by deciding for themselves how the union will act and giving instructions to the staff of the union.

Leadership also involves discipline. After every significant vote, we also had another to make it unanimous and to bind people to work towards what we had agreed and not disown the union decision. This is an important step in the process of building a sense of discipline and the unity required to fight a powerful force like Amazon.

Our achievement at BHX4 is to have built union power in the workplace against one of the most powerful capitalist organizations in the planet. Despite the recognition ballot result, the programme of workplace leader training has created a strong group of leaders who can:

- communicate with their workmates and get them to engage in collective action and collective grievances;
- use the legal right to be accompanied to represent their workmates in disciplinary and grievance meetings, and not just at BHX4, but also other Amazon sites. Because of the culture of fear, this is something that hardly ever happens in workplaces without union recognition;
- recruit others to join the union;
- work out a strategy to take the fight for recognition forward.

These workplace leaders give us real hope for the future of the union at BHX4.

6

Responding to Workers' Needs and Concerns

Many issues in a person's life can impact on their experience of work and their capacity to organize and advocate for themselves. The multifaceted states of precarity experienced by many migrants can lead to acceptance of conditions of exploitation,[1] and this has been argued by some to make migrants hard to organize, and even to lead migrant labour to become so pliable that it 'greases the wheels of the flexible labour market'.[2] Però argues that a critical factor in the success of some of the smaller 'indie' unions in organizing such workers has been their careful attention to the economic, legal, social and cultural precarity of workers' lives, responding through means such as translations, legal advice and the active involvement of members in leadership, decision making and self-representation.[3] This chapter explores these issues at BHX4, considering workers' wider conditions of life, including the distinctive challenges facing those with migrant or refugee backgrounds, and how the GMB responded.

Challenges in responding to workers' needs and concerns

This section discusses challenges that arose at BHX4 for addressing workers' diverse needs and concerns, focusing on issues that emerged concerning immigration status, English-language provision, health and family life.

As has already been noted in earlier chapters, the BHX4 workforce was highly diverse by nationality, race and immigration status.

Unsurprisingly, given Britain's hostile environment for migrants,[4] these workers therefore faced a variety of issues regarding visas and leave to remain. For example, international students seeking to transition to a sponsored work visa following the expiry of their student visa, workers seeking to bring family members to join them in the UK, and refugees approaching the end of a fixed period of leave to remain. Confidence in the English language was reported by worker-leaders as very variable among the workforce, and this was confirmed by my observations on gate jobs and picket lines.[5] According to the worker-leaders I interviewed, Amazon claimed that all of its Associates spoke good English and that therefore there was no need to translate its policies or even important safety notices – the notable exception being its decision to translate anti-union propaganda during the recognition ballot.[6] There was also evidence that this diversity among the workforce was not fully represented among managers, as this worker-leader described:

> The lack of diverse representation in leadership further alienates employees of a different background, making it challenging for our voices to resonate within a management structure disconnected from the workforce's demographic. BHX4 has a high population of workers from Eritrea and Ethiopia, however there wasn't a single person from either country above Level 1 in BHX4, the lowest tier in the Amazon hierarchy. That changed when the process for balloting on union recognition began, whereby Amazon searched the heavens and earth for an Eritrean manager to bring to BHX4, and that was ONLY to sway the vote and not to bring about diversity. (Global Majority worker-leader GA-16)

Their suggestion is that this limited Amazon's responsiveness to Global Majority workers' issues and was addressed only in a cynical move to undermine unionization. Amazon did offer its employees free ESOL classes, but worker-leaders reported that these were only available online and in workers' free time,[7] which, as noted earlier, was very limited, given the prevalence of extensive overtime and second or third jobs, and take-up was therefore unsurprisingly reported to be very low.

Health problems and Amazon's response to these – often disciplining people for time off work – was cited by multiple worker-leaders as part of their motivation for unionizing.[8] For example, one worker-leader reported:

> I had bowel cancer … Amazon said basically after four months you've now breached our policy. You have to have a … letter of concern, which is basically like me getting a written warning … It wasn't actually until I spoke to the hospital that they told me that what [Amazon has] done is illegal. It's completely breaking all rules. (European worker-leader GA-04)

Another worker-leader described:

> I was sick for a while, and I have a lump on my back, and the doctor said you don't have to go [to work] because you have stitches on the back, you have to stay home. And [Amazon] send me [to] the meeting because … according with Amazon policy, if you stay 80 hours or more [off work], they send you in the meeting, disciplinary meeting. I don't know why because I was sick. I showed the papers and … the manager at that time said to me: 'Your surgery was not mandatory.' (European Migrant worker-leader GA-21)

This lack of support from the employer for workers' health conditions compounded challenges discussed in Chapter 4 for workers supporting family members. The resulting state of bodily precarity calls to mind Judith Butler's concept of 'disposable lives' to describe those rendered vulnerable by political, social and economic systems,[9] – in this case, by Amazon's policies and management practices.

Such a diverse array of issues among members, and the interaction between multiple domains of people's lives in and out of work, gave workers many reasons to take action and seek union support. At the same time, the diversity of these concerns made it challenging to identify a particular issue that was both widely and deeply felt as a basis for collective action. Furthermore, the international backgrounds of the majority of workers created a risk that workers might compare their pay and conditions with those of workers in their country of origin rather than other workers in Britain, leading to structural inequalities between nations being reproduced in migrants' and refugees' acceptance of poor conditions in Britain.[10]

The GMB's response to meeting workers' needs and concerns

This section discusses the means by which the GMB responded to workers' concerns, beginning with the importance of informal conversations that extended the horizon of union attention far beyond immediate workplace issues to encompass anything that affected workers. The overarching ethos of the 'GMB family' is then explored, followed by its practical application to the particular needs of some workers for ESOL lessons and immigration advice.

In order to understand and respond to workers' needs and concerns, organizers and worker-leaders emphasized the importance of informal conversations, whether over the phone, by text message, on the picket line or, where possible, within the workplace.[11] An organizer explained the variety of contact they had with workers:

> [W]e had one guy ... and he was one of the original people that got people to [strike], and very respected ... He only ever came to the online meetings, but he was really helpful in getting that word out and getting information back to us on, 'This is what you need to do, this is the wording you need to use', that kind of thing. (European organizer GA-09)

A worker-leader reported: 'What has helped us is our interpersonal relationship with Associates, most of us ... were able to speak to Associates by personal contact' (Global Majority worker-leader GA-33).

Importantly, these conversations were not restricted to a narrow view of what constitutes a 'workplace issue' or 'trade union business', but took an expansive view that centred the worker and everything affecting their lives. An organizer explained:

> So even when we're not doing the striking, I'll still have casual conversations ... about their families and

what's happening, just generally in their personal life or whatever, and it's just maintaining that personal side as well to know that, 'Yeah, you're an activist or you're a leader, but we genuinely do care about you as well.' (Global Majority organizer GA-14)

The commitment to develop this further was expressed by another organizer, who said: 'what we've not done enough of [is] what you could call the whole worker organizing, which is relating all the issues in relationship to their community, citizenship, more general insecurity, their rights, what it's like to be a migrant worker in Britain, we haven't done enough of that' (European organizer GA-06).

These deep informal contacts created some challenges managing boundaries, particularly for a Global Majority organizer who described disproportionate demands from members for one-to-one support due to the level of trust and openness they had developed on the basis of their migrant background.

The GMB's conscious attempt to respond holistically to the needs and concerns of workers was expressed in the slogan of the 'GMB family'. This emerged from discussion at a strike school, as workers' way of making sense of their relationship with the union, as the following organizer described:

The big message for the strike school [was] 'What have we achieved?' [And the responses was] 'We've built a union family.' So, it's from that week of action that we started using the phrase 'union family'. That came from the strikers themselves ... Then, we were having a discussion about what next, and somebody just asked, when is Eid this year then? And then we basically repurposed an old idea. Something I've seen used on the London Underground, where you'd call a strike on the day of a football match. Not just to cause maximum chaos for the match, but also to make sure the workers get the day off to watch it. We called strikes for Eid and Orthodox Easter because they're the two main religious festivals [among the workforce at that time]. And obviously, one of the ironies of Amazon is, it employs this massive migrant labour force but doesn't make any

105

tweaking to the hours and days ... to allow them to celebrate important parts of their calendar. (European organizer GA-06)

The concept of the GMB family was thus directly connected to both workers' self-definition of what it meant to be in the union and the priority organizers placed on recognizing workers in the broader context of their lives. This clearly resonated strongly among the worker-leaders, with repeated uses of this term in meetings and interviews – for example, 'this is my first movement with the GMB family and it's really worth it' (worker-leader GA-33).

The approach expressed by the 'GMB family' helped to communicate to workers a broad interest and concern with their lives, encouraging members to come forward with a wide range of issues and providing reassurance that the union would be there to support them. This was combined with an open and welcoming attitude towards workers who had not yet joined, as this worker-leader explained:

> [Y]ou'll see people inside and you'll speak to them. You won't nag them ... but I've had conversations with people for months and months and they're like 'No, my husband said he doesn't want me to join the union' or 'No, if I gave £15 to the union, my wife would kill me'. And all those conversations. And then when you're walking down the picket line, you see them, there, they've joined ... it just makes you smile. (European organizer GA-02)

This openness supported the steady growth of union membership over time.

Within this overarching holistic approach, the union took targeted action to address some of the particular issues facing members, including the need for immigration advice and English lessons. The plans and priorities for this were discussed and developed through the weekly leaders' meetings. Organizers described their evolving orientation towards migrant rights as part of trade union practice:

> The irony in it is that everybody thinks that these migrant workers, you see these stories, are taking their

job and all this stuff. And when you actually hear the truth of it from them, it's so far away from it ... They've been sold a lie and they're stuck in this trap in this system, in the worst deprived areas within our country, in the worst poverty ... being exploited by a global giant ... And that's why now ... we're moving into a movement that's probably more about migrant rights ... and now it's about ... what could they change as migrant workers that could better themselves for working in the UK, and the conditions that they have to live in. And then it blows your brain then when you get to that point, you think: 'Oh, it's a big job.' (European organizer GA-08)

This can be seen as an evolution in trade union practice, driven by the diversification of the GMB's membership at a time of intense racism and anti-migrant politics in Britain. Further elaborating on this, another organizer made connections to aspects of state policy such as those governing access to healthcare:

[T]he immigration stuff that we were doing in the last leaders' [meeting] ... and realising ... there's so much more that affects people that we're not even touching on, that maybe we should be ... Charging people for when their children are sick ... the worry when your kids are sick anyway and then to have a £70,000 bill ... it's added stress that you don't need. (European organizer GA-09)

To help build capacity to respond to members' immigration issues, I brokered meetings between the GMB and NGOs Migrants Organise, Birmingham Citizens, Hope Projects (West Midlands), Brushstrokes and the West Midlands Immigration Advisors Network. This was informed by an understanding that unions' ability to respond to particular needs among working people – based on gender, race or migration status, for example – can be enhanced by collaborating with specialist NGOs.[12] A pilot ESOL project was launched in June 2024, in partnership with the adult education team from Birmingham City Council. As well as teaching basic English to those who needed it, this pilot also identified some members who needed support with the Secure English Language Test (SELT) qualification as part of an application for British citizenship.[13] Organizers also explored the possibility for the Amazon Workers Branch to affiliate with the Acorn tenants' union,[14] and an arrangement was made to refer members and their families to local charity Brushstrokes for accredited immigration advice.[15]

Overall, this approach embodied a deep commitment to listening to members in order to understand their concerns and priorities and find ways to respond, and to communicate to them that the union was ready to do so. This represented an expansive and open approach that corresponds to McAlevey's conception of engaging the 'whole worker'.[16] The GMB's work at BHX4 differed from some of the union's earlier initiatives (discussed in Chapter 2), in that Midlands organizers did not set out to organize migrant workers *as migrants*, but *as workers*. Then, by paying close attention to workers' needs and accessing advice from other organizations and academics about how to respond to those needs, they began to incorporate specific forms of support needed by their members – including ESOL and immigration advice – into the union's work. This has much wider relevance, given the ongoing internationalization of the workforce in many sectors, Britain's structural reliance on migrant labour, and the proliferation of migrant categories structured and positioned through multiple intersecting borders.[17]

The GMB's experience at BHX4 shows that attending to the specific needs of each worker can aid collectivization, because even where these needs do not lead to a single issue that is widely felt, this support can help workers to feel seen and heard, and in some cases the issues that are being addressed can remove barriers to further developing that individual's involvement with the union. This is particularly important when considering Mendonça's and Kougiannou's findings that insecure immigration status systematically excludes workers from membership.[18]

Approached in terms of mobility power, the recognition of the whole worker represents a radical humanization – or recognition of workers' humanity that might otherwise be neglected – that is necessary for a form of mobility that is responsive to the full dignity of a person in their social context. This represents a fundamental challenge to Amazon's instrumental and reductionist treatment of workers as simply bearers of labour power and adjuncts to machines.[19] It could thereby foster the kind of vision that can move organizing from defensive reactions to immediate issues into a struggle for social transformation.

Reflective questions for organizers, worker-leaders and activists

- What were the main challenges for the GMB responding to workers' interests and concerns at BHX4?
- How were these challenges addressed?
- What challenges do you face in responding to workers' interests and concerns in your organizing?
- How do you address these and how could you further improve?

Notes

1. Vickers, T. (2019) *Borders, Migration and Class: Producing Immigrants and Workers*, Bristol: Bristol University Press.
2. Ruhs, M. (2006) *Greasing the Wheels of the Flexible Labour Market: East European Labour Immigration in the UK*, Oxford: University of Oxford Centre on Migration, Policy and Society.
3. Però, D. (2020) 'Indie unions, organising and labour renewal: learning from precarious migrant workers', *Work, Employment and Society*, 34(5): 900–918.
4. Vickers (n1); Griffiths, M. and Yeo, C. (2021) 'The UK's hostile environment: deputising immigration control', *Critical Social Policy*, 41(4): 521–544; Bhattacharyya, G. (2023) *The Futures of Racial Capitalism*, London: Polity.
5. Fieldnotes 10 January 2024, 13 February 2024.
6. Fieldnotes 24 June 2024.
7. Fieldnotes 17 January 2024.
8. Interviews GA-01, GA-04, GA-07 and GA-21.
9. Butler, J. (2020) *Precarious Life: The Powers of Mourning and Violence*, London: Verso.
10. Vickers (n1).
11. Fieldnotes 18 June 2024.
12. Schmidt, E. (2005) 'Coalition building: trade union dialogues with civil society', *Transfer*, 11(3): 449–456.
13. Fieldnotes 5 June 2024.
14. Fieldnotes 28 February 2024.
15. Fieldnotes 5 August 2024.
16. McAlevey, J.F. (2016) *No Shortcuts: Organizing for Power*, Oxford: Oxford University Press, p 28.

[17] Vickers (n 1); Mezzadra, S. and Neilson, B. (2013) *Border as Method, or, the Multiplication of Labour*, Durham, NC: Duke University Press.

[18] Mendonça, P. and Kougiannou, N.K. (2024) ' "We are not all the same": the capacity of different groups of food delivery gig workers to build collective and individual power resources', *Work, Employment and Society*, DOI:10.1177/09500170241257437.

[19] Kassem, S. (2023) *Work and Alienation in the Platform Economy: Amazon and the Power of Organisation*, Bristol: Bristol University Press.

Applying Personal Experience and Community Work in Organizing at Amazon

Ferdousara Uddin, GMB Regional Organizer

I moved to the UK aged four years old, with my mother and two older siblings. This was the first time my mother had left her village, let alone the country. We came to live with my dad who had already been in the UK since the early 1970s. Growing up as a minority in Stoke-on-Trent, as one of the couple-of-hundred South Asian families you were a part of a tight-knit community. Our first home was living in the flat above our family restaurant alongside other staff members.

As soon as I had mastered the basic English language, I was promoted to being a translator for my parents, from answering the phone, going to GP/hospital appointments with my mother, reading and translating letters, and filling in forms.

Stoke was not a friendly and safe place for migrants, racist attacks were common, and the black and ethnic community were a minority in the city. Living in a very tight knit community, you live through the hardship of being a foreigner in an unknown land, but as a child, it then becomes the norm of seeing the divide of race. You grow up surrounded by a distrust of officials, of outsiders because you overhear whispered words of deportation, of uncles 'hiding', of families being separated.

You feel the fear following the aftermath of a racist attack on a restaurant or someone in the community, but you see how powerless the community are and the acceptance of these attacks knowing that there will be no support, and how no one will reach out to the police with an understanding that it is pointless, especially in the 1980s when the far right terrorized the streets on a regular basis.

My father spent all his free time helping his fellow countrymen to integrate into the community and making a space for the South Asian community. At the age of 13, I was taking minutes so that people like my father did not feel at a disadvantage and unable to have an active role because of language barriers. The Bangladeshi families created their own network to keep their culture and heritage, but also supporting one another, everyone became your 'cousin'.

I became a member of the Racial Equality Council at the age of 14, because even though we second-generation migrants spoke impeccable English and had integrated into the country, the racism we faced continued. I knew it could only be challenged and changed if those experiencing it were part of this.

My mother still has traditional and cultural values, like many of the other aunties who came into this country. They acquired the invaluable skills of being a homemaker, but never implemented them outside of those four walls. I went on to be one of the founders of the Bangladeshi Women's Association, this group empowered women to get together away from their traditional and cultural roles of being a housewife and collectively organize themselves to undertake projects and events.

It was a natural transition to become a community development worker. Our office was a base for local residents who were able drop in to seek support with filling in forms, community groups applying for grants, and working with the local government in how their budget should be utilized to help the local areas. The community were mainly working-class people living on the poverty line and overlooked. One of the redevelopment projects I led involved two local parks. The residents were empowered to make the decision in how the recreational area should be used by them and their families.

In my own personal life, I married at 21, broke cultural norms and did not have an arranged marriage. I married into an extremely orthodox religious family, where women were confined by cultural practices and lived a completely different life from the one I grew up in. It was an oppressive and abusive marriage that led to a divorce 15 years later, and here I experienced the full force of the South Asian reproach. Domestic abuse is still taboo within the South Asian community, and I truly understood how embedded cultural beliefs are even in the UK.

When I became Charities Lead for Centrica Women's Network and attended a workshop led by Women's Aid, I realized that companies can choose to have a policy to support their employees experiencing domestic abuse. I knew from my own experience within the company that this was a campaign that had to be led. Working closely with external organizations, Centrica's Domestic Abuse Policy was launched in November 2021. Alongside support for employees, a campaign was launched to help British Gas customers too.

I became involved in the GMB after experiencing frustration at the lack of support from my then-union. I was already supporting colleagues as well as representing myself, so within 12 months of being elected as a union rep, I became a full-time employed union official. This was November 2022, when we had just lost a ballot for industrial action at Amazon BHX4 by three votes.

I joined the Amazon campaign as someone who had never been involved with Amazon before, so I needed to find my feet first. It became apparent from being on the gate jobs that even though we were doing everything to communicate with the workers, they were not hearing us. In those early days, our approach felt unnatural to me because it was a way that I had never communicated before. I recall a GMB pamphlet with so much information that was union jargon – the question I asked was: 'Do they need to know all this?' We stripped it all back and started creating videos and voicenotes, simplifying what a union is. We began to change the way we communicated, so finally members not only heard us but also understood us.

When I started joining the pickets, I instantly struck a connection with the workers. For many of them, striking was an alien concept and they needed someone to lead them – but it had to be someone they could speak to, trust and who they felt would understand them.

Trust comes in many ways, but if you connect with someone through cultural or religious beliefs, or life experiences, you are more likely to be receptive, and that's what happened on the picket line. I became their sister, so when I led them on a march, they trusted me in my actions and followed. I was able to find the leaders on the picket line, encourage and empower them to take control of their picket.

When I found those organic leaders, I knew how important it was to maintain that relationship, so communication was key. By having individual conversations, by supporting them through their own personal cases, I was able to ask questions where many wouldn't have been able to. Through these conversations we were able to discover individual and collective issues.

'Amanah' – in Islam this word refers to someone entrusting you with something and leaving it in your possession. That is what the Amazon workers have given me. I am in a privileged position in which they have entrusted me, and for me it is more important than ever to maintain the relationship because the fight goes on.

7

Building Wider Support

Wider support, from people who are not directly subject to an employer's discipline but who can exert influence on the company, can strengthen workers' ability to meet their demands. Doellgast, Bidwell and Colvin identify a growing trend among trade unions internationally, as traditional institutions have weakened, to pursue strategies that can challenge employers' claim to legitimacy and threaten reputational backlash as a point of leverage.[1] Wider support can also make a material difference to workers' ability to sustain action. Due to the importance of the strike hardship payments outlined in Chapter 4, a wider movement that can consistently raise donations seems essential if the organizing model described here were to extend to other sites and realize its potential for sustained action.

McAlevey's approach to building wider support begins with the power structure analysis, which identifies both potential organic allies for unionized workers by looking at the 'whole worker' and their multiple social connections, and institutions beyond the company where pressure might be brought, whether through the employer's investors, partners, consumers or regulators. These are areas where Holgate argues that the newer 'indie' unions in the UK have generally done better than traditional unions like the GMB.[2] This chapter examines challenges the GMB faced as it tried to build wider support with the BHX4 workers, and how the union responded.

Challenges in building wider support

This section explores the challenges building wider support, rooted in the wider political conditions in Britain during this period.

115

The Coventry experience demonstrates the continuing relevance of Gall's observation that greater resources are needed for unionizing in sectors of the 'new economy' that involve 'products and services being produced and delivered in historically relatively innovative ways using recent developments in information and communication technologies'.[3] This increases the need to deploy resources strategically and with a focus on employers that have wider social significance. A strong argument can be made for Amazon as a candidate for such strategic commitment of resources because, as Delfanti argues, Amazon's concentrated economic power 'means that it has the ability to deeply influence the way in which we work', with other companies adopting 'similar technologies in their attempt to catch up with Amazon and uproot the company from its dominant position in the market'.[4] This calls for a focused union response, as opposed to spreading resources more thinly across many different employers, and the development of a wider movement of support to sustain this.

One of the major challenges in developing such a wider movement was the relative weakness of social movement infrastructure or activity in Britain during the period under discussion, with the notable exception of movements in solidarity with Palestine since October 2023.[5] This low ebb for progressive social movements has its historical roots in the defeat of the anti-war movement in 2003 and the student movement against cuts and fees in 2010.[6] Much of Britain's activist left, which was already quite limited when considered from a historical and international perspective, was absorbed into the Labour Party during Jeremy Corbyn's leadership from 2015 to 2019,[7] and then expelled under its new party leader Keir Starmer, leading to fragmentation and demoralization. While movements later developed under the banner of Black Lives Matter in 2020, Palestine solidarity in 2021 and intermittent climate activism, none of these gave rise to the kind of broader progressive institutions that would have been capable of supporting a national campaign on Amazon. Furthermore, Holgate highlights the relatively weak tradition of labour/community alliances in the UK,[8] arguing that this makes it more difficult to build new alliances.

The conditions for a wider movement around BHX4 also differed markedly from previous attempts to build community–union alliances in the UK, limiting the potential for transferable lessons.

For example, the recent notable example of the 'Community' wing of Unite the Union, which was established in 2011 with the aim of organizing pensioners, students and the unemployed, originated from a recognition of the failures of the Labour Party, the difficulties in taking industrial action in many critical sectors such as the NHS, the strength of the student movement on the streets, and the awareness of the disenfranchised young unemployed.[9] The attempt to build community alliances at BHX4 was very different, with an active strike wave but limited street movements involving other sections of society.

This posed a significant challenge when attempting to learn from earlier periods of struggle in the UK or to apply McAlevey's approach that was developed in the context of the US, where there are much stronger established practices and infrastructures for long-term alliance building. For example, with particular reference to organizing in relation to Amazon, Olney and Wilson discuss the Awood Centre, founded by a partnership between the Council on American-Islamic Relations Minnesota Chapter and the Service Employees International Union (SEIU) union, which employed Somali community organizers and secured improvements in working conditions.[10] In another example, Kaoosji discusses the creation of the San Bernadino Airport Communities coalition in 2019,[11] which ultimately defeated a regional development plan that the coalition said would have expanded Amazon's operations at the expense of having 'displaced thousands of residents ... accelerated the creation of poverty level employment, taken away much needed housing from residents in the project zone and added to the already severely high levels of air pollution the region suffers from'.[12]

These challenges help to explain the limited mobilization of support for the BHX4 workers. As an organizer commented: 'It's big news, it's on the telly, people know about Amazon ... But we haven't made it, give a fiver a week to the Amazon Strikers kind of campaign ... And painting that picture of "This is a battle for the entire future of work"' (European organizer GA-06).

Yet, despite these challenges, Johnson and Herman argue that in Britain, 'there are increasing opportunities, and incentives, for a plurality of social partners to form alliances and coalitions around broader social justice concerns',[13] and emphasize the importance of traditional trade unions within such alliances. The BHX4 campaign shows early indications of how those opportunities might be realized, and which could be further built on.

The GMB's response to build wider support

This section examines how the GMB built wider support for the BHX4 workers, beginning with the successes of a local Amazon Workers Support Group and then considering the support provided by the TUC, NGOs, the Labour Party, academics and international coalitions.

The most sustained source of support for the BHX4 workers beyond the GMB came from an Amazon Workers Support Group established in Coventry with the support of Coventry Trades Council and various small British left-wing political groups, as an organizer explained:

> We've deliberately set up a support group, which is explicitly modelled on … what they had in the miners' strike [of 1984–1985] … That support group have raised a hell of a lot of money for the dispute … they get people down on the picket line … they're not just signing a cheque from a union branch meeting … they're getting support from properly representative meetings of workers … The issue with the solidarity strategy … is, it's a lot harder to sustain a strike of a thousand people with strike pay than it is a hundred … If your model is 'Let's build something like the miners support groups', we've got one miners' support group in one pit village … we haven't got people collecting outside workplaces and supermarkets every day for the strike fund. (European organizer GA-06)

This support group was thus limited by its geographical and social reach, yet still played an important part and demonstrated an initial step that could be built on.

Support also came from many other sources. The TUC, a federation of trade unions to which the GMB is affiliated, also supported the BHX4 workers, particularly in the period leading up to the recognition ballot, by providing training, personnel and software to strengthen worker-leaders' ability to communicate by text with many members at once,[14] and by running a publicity campaign across Coventry and Birmingham involving paid advertising at bus stops encouraging BHX4 workers to vote 'Yes' for recognition. Further support was provided by an NGO, Foxglove, including extensive pro bono legal support, particularly in relation to the recognition ballot, and local charity Brushstrokes, including free accredited immigration advice to GMB members and their families. Academics also contributed, for example, by examining and publicizing working conditions, providing research to help inform union strategy, and documenting and evaluating the organizing process to inform its further development. In August 2024 a new institution was created to coordinate these academic contributions through a Work Futures Observatory, co-funded by the GMB and Nottingham Trent University.

Through the GMB's affiliation to the Labour Party, the union sought to influence policies to improve working conditions and make it easier for workers to unionize. The Amazon Workers Midlands Branch, which included BHX4, brought motions to the GMB National Congress in 2023 and 2024 calling for union access to be made a condition of public procurement contracts, and in 2024 a second motion calling for reform of the CAC process for union recognition.[15] On 9 September 2024, the GMB presented a briefing in Parliament using the BHX4 recognition process and the research in this book as a case study.[16] Eight out of the ten proposals made in that briefing were incorporated into the first draft of the Employment Rights Bill that followed.[17] This political engagement was further supported by extensive media work involving regional and national GMB officers to raise public awareness of Amazon's employment practices and the workers' struggle.

Challenging Amazon's international reach, the GMB built relationships of mutual support, for example, as part of the Make Amazon Pay Coalition and the UNI Global Union Amazon Alliance. In November 2023, BHX4 workers played a leading role in coordinated strikes and protests in more than 30 countries, timed to coincide with the company's 'Black Friday' sale, and during the first half of 2024, trade unionists travelled from the US, Germany and Ireland to support the BHX4 workers. This international support was further strengthened by a letter from a group of investors representing over $1.2 trillion in assets under management or advice, calling on the company to recognize the GMB at BHX4.[18]

These strategies to build wider support have wide relevance because they offer a means to build power within those public, private and community spaces, from the streets to state institutions to people's homes, which Amazon does not control, but must move through and interact with in the course of its business.

While the initiatives discussed here go far beyond what is common for British trade union campaigns of this period, the building of wider support was arguably less developed compared to other parts of the GMB's campaign at BHX4, which has consequently required a shorter chapter. This partly reflects the deliberate prioritization of workplace organization by the GMB as the main foundation of the union's strength, but it also shows room for further development, whether by the GMB or by other organizations in support of its campaign.

Reflective questions for organizers, worker-leaders and activists

- What were the main challenges for the GMB building wider support with the workers at BHX4?
- How were these challenges addressed?
- What challenges do you face building wider support in your organizing?
- How do you address these and how could you further improve?

Notes

[1] Doellgast, V., Bidwell, M. and Colvin, A.J.S. (2021) 'New directions in employment relations theory: understanding fragmentation, identity, and legitimacy', *ILR Review*, 74(3): 555–579.
[2] Holgate, J. (2021) *Arise: Power, Strategy and Union Resurgence*, London: Pluto Press.
[3] Gall, G. (2005) 'Organizing non-union workers as trade unionists in the "new economy" in Britain', *Economic and Industrial Democracy*, 26(1): 41–63, at 44.
[4] Delfanti, A. (2021) *The Warehouse: Workers and Robots at Amazon*, London: Pluto Press, p 8.
[5] Fekete, L. (2024) 'Anti-Palestinian racism and the criminalisation of international solidarity in Europe', *Race & Class*, 66(1): 99–120.

[6] Rios-Jara, H. (2021) 'From revolt to reform: student protests and the higher education agenda in England 2009–2019', in L. Cini, D. della Porta and C. Guzmán-Concha (eds) *Student Movements in Late Neoliberalism: Social Movements and Transformation*, Cham: Palgrave Macmillan, pp 213–239.

[7] Vickers, T. (2019) *Borders, Migration and Class: Producing Immigrants and Workers*, Bristol: Bristol University Press.

[8] Holgate, J. (2015) 'An international study of trade union involvement in community organising: same model, different outcomes', *British Journal of Industrial Relations*, 53(2): 460–483.

[9] Holgate, J. (2021) 'Trade unions in the community: building broad spaces of solidarity', *Economic and Industrial Democracy*, 42(2): 226–247.

[10] Olney, P. and Wilson, R. (2020) 'Think big: organising a successful Amazon workers' movement in the United States by combining the strengths of the left and organised labor', in J. Alimahomed-Wilson and E. Reese (eds) *The Cost of Free Shipping: Amazon in the Global Economy*, London: Pluto Press, pp 250–264.

[11] Kaoosji, S. (2020) 'Worker and community organising to challenge Amazon's algorithmic threat', in J. Alimahomed-Wilson and E. Reese (eds) *The Cost of Free Shipping: Amazon in the Global Economy*, London: Pluto Press, pp 194–205.

[12] SB Airport Communities (no date) [online], Available from: https://sbairportcommunities.org/ [Accessed 11 November 2024).

[13] Johnson, M. and Herman, E. (2024) 'Out with the old, in with the new? Institutional experimentation and decent work in the UK', *Economic and Industrial Democracy*, DOI:10.1177/0143831X23 1220528, at 17.

[14] Fieldnotes 18 June 2024.

[15] Fieldnotes 10 June 2024.

[16] GMB (2024) 'The GMB campaign for trade union recognition in Amazon Coventry' [online], Available form: https://www.gmb.org.uk/assets/media/documents/the-gmb-union-campaign-for-trade-union-recognition-in-amazon-coventry-bleed.pdf [Accessed 8 November 2024].

[17] UK Parliament (2024) 'Employment Rights Bill' [online], Available from: https://publications.parliament.uk/pa/bills/cbill/59-01/0011/240011.pdf [Accessed 11 November 2024].

[18] CCLA (2024) '50 investors write to Amazon in relation to workers' rights to organise', [online], Available from: https://www.ccla.co.uk/news-media/50-investors-write-amazon-relation-workers-rights-organise [Accessed 16 July 2024].

ESSAY 9

Why We Need an International Alliance Against Amazon

Garfield Hylton, GMB worker-leader at BHX4

Amazon is a giant operating in many countries, creating its vast wealth from consumers and from governments by selling Web services. The company continues to grow and make acquisitions that give them market dominance. Their financial power allows them to dictate to workers and governments.

The GMB operates in the UK as a single membership entity. Our experience of Amazon's union-busting tactics showed that no single entity could curtail Amazon's restless pursuit of exploitation. We don't have the same financial power as Amazon and it soon became clear that making Amazon pay would require an alliance and pooling resources, sharing strategies and showing solidarity. During our strikes, we were supported by Uni Global Union, who would forge strong links with the GMB. Uni Global Union is a true global organization working to support workers across the world.

This evolving process has seen BHX4 Coventry workers bring the spotlight to Amazon and create an effective partnership that has united 50 unions from 20-plus countries such as Brazil, the US, Germany, Italy, Poland, India, Spain, Australia, Austria and more. As an Amazon worker and GMB rep, I have been fortunate to have the opportunity to contribute to this, including speaking at events concerning the climate, Black workers' events, three trade union conferences and NGOs. The year 2024 saw GMB officers travel with myself to the US to meet with the Teamsters and Amazon workers at Staten Island.

This partnership working has allowed for a greater awareness about the physical and mental toll of Amazon's high productivity-driven pace, accompanied by constant overzealous surveillance. This information was shared across the world's media. November 24, 2023 saw the greatest international show of solidarity to date in the 'Make Amazon Pay' campaign, when Amazon workers and their allies in 30 countries staged actions which overshadowed Amazon's 'Black Friday' campaign.

Amazon is being attacked on many fronts, and the political campaign team have assisted in the motion that was created at last year's GMB Conference that was put to the then leader of the Labour Party Sir Keir Stammer. We are hoping that the Employment Rights Bill will be passed to prevent the likes of Amazon being able to interfere with a due democratic process of workers organizing to form a union.

A German Amazon worker who visited us in Coventry said:

> Every day we face the same challenges in Amazon warehouses. Low wages, high stress and lack of respect for our rights. Joining this global day of action is not just about us in Germany, but standing together with our colleagues worldwide to demand fair treatment. We want Amazon to hear us loud and clear: it's time to make changes for the better.

With many organizations coming together and coordinating actions across the globe in the fight to 'Make Amazon Pay', it is hoped that workers take renewed vigour and confidence that their voices are being heard. Their actions speak louder than words, and now the worldwide audience understands the cost of shopping at Amazon, for humans and the environment.

8

Principles of the Coventry Model

Drawing together the analysis presented in Chapters 3–7, this chapter presents six key principles that express the most distinctive aspects of the GMB's approach at BHX4 and that have particular relevance to organizing workplaces where unions have limited access to the workplace. These are summed up as the six C's of the Coventry Model: *Capitalize, Create, Cultivate, Connect, Challenge,* and *Contest.*

1. *Capitalize* on spontaneous ruptures in the employer's control

- The self-organized protests in August 2022 represented a moment of unity around a deeply felt injustice of pay that prompted mass direct action. This temporarily ruptured Amazon's control over the space of the warehouse, when workers turned the canteen into a protest site, and the company's control over workers' time, when they refused to return to work at the end of their break. Amazon's attempt to reimpose discipline by clocking workers off and thereby withholding their pay led to further ruptures as workers moved into the more autonomous space of the streets. By setting the workers into motion under their own direction, this created momentum. The rapid mobilization of GMB organizers in response to these ruptures was equally critical. It was effective because organizers paid close attention to what workers were saying and positioned the union as a vehicle for their struggle, prioritizing the issue that mattered to them and offering the legal protections of official strike action to continue the workers' momentum. The GMB was only in a position to respond in this way because of consistent but unglamorous casework and campaigning over the previous decade that built trusting relationships with a small group of workers and provided a foundation for a rapid expansion of the membership.

- Applying this principle elsewhere requires an awareness that it is often impossible to predict exactly where and when such ruptures will occur, but history demonstrates that they are a recurring feature of capitalism and can therefore be prepared for. Broad and steady work across different employers and sectors increases the chances that a union will have relevant contacts at the site of any rupture. Addressing issues that matter to workers, using methods such as casework, grievances and campaigning, can build relationships of trust and workers' identification with the union that then enables the union to respond when there is a sudden rupture. The issues involved in this steady preparatory work may only affect a minority, or even a single worker, but can still build the relationships that enable the union to respond when a broader unifying issue emerges. A critical task here is identifying when to move from slow and steady preparatory work across many employers to a focused and rapid concentration of resources on a single target to capitalize on a moment of rupture in the employer's control, and ensuring that all organizers are brought along in this shift in pace and focus.

2. *Create* democratic spaces and times outside the employers' control

- GMB organizers built on the temporary ruptures in Amazon's control that were caused by the wildcat walkouts by creating, together with workers, autonomous times and spaces where workers could associate more freely and engage in democratic discussion, education and decision making, and where organizers could associate with workers and identify natural leaders. Spaces created during strike times, such as pickets, strike schools and mass meetings, played a crucial role. Workers' ability to move autonomously within these spaces, stepping outside Amazon's control, was enabled by the union's hardship payments. This engendered discussion of strategy and tactics that gave space to everybody, including workers and organizers, to bring their contributions and have them taken seriously. Workers' in-depth knowledge of the labour process at BHX4, their contact with other workers and their understanding of the wider context of workers' lives were thereby brought together with the legal, organizational and historical knowledge among the organizing team. A strong expectation was established that everybody should contribute to discussion and decision making, supported by the consistent line from organizers that the workers were the union and that the struggle belonged to them.

- The need to create autonomous times and spaces outside the employer's control has wide relevance, although the exact means by which this principle can be applied will be highly dependent on context. In situations where workers have sufficient free time and live in close enough proximity, it may be easier to gather workers in person outside of strike time, but where workers are working long hours, potentially across multiple jobs, and travelling long distances to their workplace, the protected time of strikes supported by hardship payments may be vital to build democratic participation. Of course, there may also be possibilities to organize virtually, but none of the virtual organizing spaces I witnessed among BHX4 workers, whether WhatsApp groups or video calls, came close to the level of mass participation and collective confidence that was evident in workers' in-person gatherings.

3. *Cultivate* worker-leadership through deep support and education

- The GMB's regional and national structures enabled deep support for worker-leaders at BHX4, extending far beyond Amazon's control. This was vital given the power that Amazon held over worker-leaders via the employer's control over pay, hours, disciplinary measures, and role and task allocation. Worker-leaders within the GMB came under intense pressure within the workplace, but received support through the leaders' days, mentoring and other one-to-one support from GMB organizers, and from personal visits and meetings with senior officials at the regional and national levels. In some cases, this was further extended spatially, for example, through worker-leaders' involvement in local, national and international meetings, all supported by union funding for expenses and loss of pay. This support that worker-leaders received outside the warehouse strengthened their ability to operate as leaders within the highly controlled space of the workplace and during their working hours, knowing that they would have the support of organizers in the event that they were victimized. It also strengthened their ability to use their contact with other workers in the warehouse strategically, informed by mapping and planning of the workplace during strike schools and leaders' days.

• In considering the wider application of this principle, it is important to bear in mind that support for worker-leaders at BHX4 came in multiple forms. This included both spaces for worker-leaders to form as a community and support one another, and support from organizers and other parts of the GMB structure. It was both a collective and individual process that took account of each worker-leader's particular qualities and the role they were willing to play. It also accounted for the many other pressures in worker-leaders' lives by offering flexibility in attendance and financial support for expenses and loss of earnings. Fundamentally, this highlights the value of a wider structure capable of supporting a particular struggle, and the importance of engaging worker-leaders actively with this structure as well as with each other.

4. *Connect* with workers' lives beyond the workplace

• By showing care for the wider times and places of workers' lives, which in many cases extended internationally, the GMB provided a fundamentally different alternative compared to Amazon's conditional use of workers for their labour power. This was expressed in the idea of the 'GMB family' and concretely developed through referral arrangements for immigration advice and ESOL lessons. Underpinning this was an understanding that all parts of a person's life are interconnected and that therefore even issues that occur in other times and spaces away from the workplace have a bearing on a worker's power vis-à-vis their employer. The application of this principle strengthened workers' ability to engage in union activities at BHX4, deepened their sense of identity with the union, and laid the basis for alliances between the GMB and organizations specializing in issues such as migrant rights and housing.

- When applying this principle in other settings, it is important to emphasize that both the overall framing and the particular issues taken up by the GMB were not predetermined, but emerged through extensive discussions between workers and organizers in the autonomous spaces discussed earlier and through numerous informal conversations wherever opportunities presented themselves. The core of this principle is therefore close attention to what workers are saying, combined with the creation of spaces in which to discuss and a presentation of the union as interested in any issue that affects a worker, even if it has no obvious connection to the workplace. This resonates with long traditions of diaspora thinking and practice.

5. *Challenge* the employer's freedom to operate

- The GMB's BHX4 campaign extended far beyond the workplace to the wider context in which the company had to operate. The union engaged diverse actors who had influence over Amazon's practices, including the public via its media work, Labour Party politicians, the CAC and the legal system. Much of this was done in collaboration with other organizations, such as the TUC and NGOs. Although it is difficult to prove the full consequences of this activity with certainty, it seems likely to have influenced the policing of strikes, due to the political consequences for the police if they were seen to be defending Amazon's widely reported poor employment practices, and to have contributed to increased trade union access through the 2024 Employment Rights Bill.
- The application of this principle to other contexts centres on the recognition that while union access to a workplace may be limited, most employers must operate in a wider environment that they cannot control so tightly, and where there will be other actors – whether the state, customers or other campaigning organizations – that might help to bring pressure to bear.

6. *Contest* employer control of the workplace

- Worker-leaders and organizers at BHX4 showed great creativity in finding ways to contest Amazon's control over workers' movements within the space and time of work. These varied from the use of QR codes on the backs of worker-leaders' phones to enable colleagues to join the union and answer surveys, to conversations in the canteen and smoking shelters, to interventions using company structures such as the Associate Forum, VOA Board, and Team Connect and All-Hands meetings, to the use of individual and collective grievance procedures, to informal verbal challenges to managers, and to temporary work stoppages. This all contributed to what was widely described as a changed atmosphere inside the warehouse, including more contact between workers and greater confidence to challenge managers. The growth of GMB membership ultimately enabled an application for formal recognition, which if successful would have contested Amazon's control of the warehouse at an even more fundamental level by providing a legal basis for increased rights for the union within the warehouse and a requirement for Amazon to negotiate over a range of crucial aspects of its employment practices.

• The experience of the GMB at BHX4 demonstrates that even in a highly controlled workplace with a precarious workforce and an employer that is hostile to unionization, there are opportunities to contest the employer's control. These spaces can be used creatively to support organizing, and as organizing progresses, these spaces for contestation can be further expanded using both formal and informal means.

These principles are particularly relevant to organizing in conditions where unions have limited access to the workplace. At BHX4, the GMB were not permitted access, so they created it. These principles also have wider importance, given the increasing prevalence of conditions of employment that Mezzadra and Neilson sum up as involving: intensification – evident at Amazon in the enforced pace of work; diversification – evident at Amazon in the array of tasks and roles within the warehouse; and heterogenization – evident at Amazon in the varied configurations of international familial relations, cultural and linguistic milieux, and immigration statuses among the workforce.[1] The Coventry Model shows effective ways to grapple with the fragmented temporal and spatial configurations that these conditions produce, and the precarious and constrained yet highly differentiated forms of movement that are increasingly prevalent in today's crisis-ridden world.[2]

Reflective question for organizers, worker-leaders and activists

Consider each of the six C's of the Coventry Model in turn (*Capitalize, Create, Cultivate, Connect, Challenge* and *Contest*): how might you be able to apply each of these in your own organizing?

Notes

[1] Mezzadra, S. and Neilson, B. (2013) *Border as Method, or, the Multiplication of Labour*, Durham, NC: Duke University Press.
[2] Vickers, T. (2019) *Borders, Migration and Class: Producing Immigrants and Workers*, Bristol: Bristol University Press.

9

Conclusion

The GMB's BHX4 campaign represents a huge step forward for trade unionism faced with the changing nature of work and the changing composition of the working class. It challenges the idea that traditional trade unions cannot undertake such organizing effectively, demonstrating that they can be just as capable of fostering the kind of 'communities of struggle' that Però identifies as critical to the success of indie unions organizing precarious workers.[1] The principles identified in Chapter 8 as constituting the Coventry Model show how this was achieved at BHX4, although it is important to also take into account other factors beyond the union's control that contributed to the growth of membership, including the combined pressures on workers that prompted the first mass actions in August 2022, and a management culture that worker-leaders consistently described as disrespectful, irritating many workers and pushing them towards the union.

The analysis presented here is not intended to claim that trade unions following these principles will always and everywhere be able to achieve the same results (falling into the formulaic trap that Little, Sharp, Stevenson and Will warn against),[2] but rather that the Coventry Model offers lessons for how to make the most of the opportunities that present themselves; in particular, how to capitalize on, and create, spaces and times for organizing as a mobile practice in environments that are highly controlled by an employer that is hostile to autonomous worker organizing. This offers a practical and applied example of a broader point I have made elsewhere[3] about the need to account for objective and subjective factors in order to build working-class power. This also needs to take into account that the long-term crisis of capitalism repeatedly creates the objective conditions for such action to be possible, but that trade unions and other working-class organizations need to be ready to seize the time and respond as soon as opportunities present themselves. The GMB is already applying the lessons from the Coventry Model elsewhere, for example, in its equal pay campaign at Birmingham City Council, where the union built a Communications Action Network of worker-leaders, and in building power among British Gas workers.

Looking ahead, there are several possible avenues that the GMB and other unions might pursue to further build on the Coventry Model. First, the search for organic leaders at BHX4 mainly involved organizers seeking leaders among existing GMB members, and this was highly effective. The next step, which the GMB has already started to pursue, is to educate worker-leaders in this approach, and for them to actively seek to identify, speak with and win over organic leaders within the workplace who have not yet joined the union. The kind of systematic face-to-face surveys advocated by McAlevey could help here in terms of understanding the issues that are of most concern to organic leaders outside the union.[4] Although the arrangement of work in Amazon makes this difficult, the accounts of worker-leaders suggest there are opportunities for some such discussions, for example, in the canteen, and the potential for worker-leaders to engage other workers further with QR codes leading to online surveys set up by organizers. This also raises the question of how to further deepen the understanding and confidence of worker-leaders who have emerged through the Amazon campaign. The GMB passed a motion at its 2024 Congress committing the union to further develop its support for the lifelong learning of members, providing a strong mandate to pursue this.

Looking beyond the workplace, while the GMB has already applied part of McAlevey's 'whole worker' concept,[5] in addressing members' needs for ESOL and immigration advice, more might be done to apply the more political aspect of the 'whole worker' approach by engaging worker-leaders in a systematic mapping of their networks and communities outside of work to identify natural allies who might be brought into an alliance against Amazon. This connects with traditions of powerful worker–community alliances in the UK, which have often begun with workers' families as a first step and ongoing central pillar.[6] Allinson explores various ways of conducting this kind of mapping as part of a power structure analysis, in ways that enrich workers' understanding about power and influence.[7] This could also be assisted by further developing the relationships with organizations the GMB has met in the course of the BHX4 campaign, such as Migrants Organise and Birmingham Citizens. Based on a review of such alliances in the UK, the US and Australia, Holgate highlights the importance of 'practical issues of "fit" between the ideology and culture of a union and its coalition partners, and the way in which structures and patterns of practice enable, or not, a full engagement of unions within a coalition'.[8] This suggests that careful selection of partners and long-term investment in relationship building are critical, alongside investment in education and training among all members of the alliance to nurture a shared understanding.

Building alliances and public support might also be aided by developing a discursive framing that connects the Amazon workers' struggle to issues of broad concern among the public, adopting the kind of approach that was successful in building support for rail workers in 2022 through the questions that the National Union of Rail, Maritime and Transport Workers (RMT union) posed about the social distribution of wealth.[9] In the case of Amazon, this might involve connecting with public anxiety about the displacement of human agency by AI and robots, or otherwise connecting with broader questions about the kind of society we want to live in, potentially using this as a motivation to donate a small amount to the Amazon workers' strike fund whenever people buy from the company. This could strengthen the sustainability of the Coventry Model and raise funds for its extension to other sites. The extension of the GMB's campaign to other sites would also make it more difficult for Amazon to concentrate so many resources in one place, as it was able to do when the recognition ballot was running only at BHX4.

The GMB could build on its referral arrangements to immigration advice and ESOL, which are extremely valuable but arguably limited to a service model of trade unionism, by also engaging in migrants rights work as part of the union's organizing model. This could involve directly challenging the immigration laws that deepen workers' precarity and limit their rights, rendering them more vulnerable to exploitation.[10] Such a stance could encourage solidarity by directing attention towards the structures of the capitalist state that divide workers. There is precedence for this – for example, in July

2019, protests took place in eight cities in the US against Amazon's collaboration with immigration enforcement against its workers.[11] This would represent an organic evolution from the issues raised by GMB members in their struggle at BHX4, as part of a grassroots political trade unionism as advocated by Holgate and Little, Sharp, Stevenson and Winter.[12]

The GMB's experience at BHX4 and the analysis of that experience presented here have implications for the theorization of labour exploitation and resistance through a mobility lens. It highlights the importance of creating temporal-spatial configurations that empower workers to resist the relentless productivity demanded by their employer and reclaim their autonomy of mobility – for example, through mass strikes and leadership training programmes. The work of trade union organizers can be seen as a form of mobility-as-practice that is autonomous from capitalist labour discipline and thereby capable of supporting an expansion of mobility power among workers. Importantly, this involves democratic organizing and ceding of some power by organizers to workers – which can be seen as a form of 'moving with', a fundamentally different relationship to the Amazon–employee relation which can be expressed as a regimented 'movement under discipline'. It also represents a break from the dynamics of service unionism, which might be conceptualized as 'moving for', or of advocacy unionism, which might be seen as 'moving on behalf of'. In this, the resources and size of the GMB have been shown to enable rather than constrain the autonomy of mobility of workers and worker-leaders at BHX4. The findings here suggest that traditional trade unions still have considerable potential, where they are prepared to genuinely listen to workers and transform their practices in response to the lessons they learn from them. Considering Però's definition of 'indie' unions as 'independent grassroots unions co-led by precarious migrant workers',[13] to the extent that precarious migrant workers exercise co-leadership in their struggle through the GMB, we must ask whether the distinction between 'indie' and 'traditional' unions loses its significance. The force of this argument is further increased by noting that the Coventry Model embodies many of the other characteristics Però suggests have contributed to indie unions' success, such as agility, imagination, attentiveness to members' needs and the willingness to confront employers without waiting for recognition or a supermajority.

This book demonstrates why the reforms to union access and recognition proposed in the 2024 Employment Rights Bill are so essential, and at the same time shows that impediments to access can be multiple and complex, extending beyond formal rights. It is worth bearing in mind here examples from other countries which demonstrate that greater formal rights via the state do not necessarily translate into an empowered workforce. For example, Massimo describes France's state-mandated workers' elections in Amazon warehouses and collective bargaining at a company level, yet combining with low levels of trade union membership, typically at around 5–10 per cent in a given Amazon warehouse, and periodic strikes struggling to mobilize as many as 100 workers in a given warehouse.[14] In Italy, an initial period of industrial action from the autumn of 2017 combined with a media campaign and government support to force Amazon to negotiate with the unions. However, Massimo argues that this brought little improvement on many issues that were important concerns for the workers, including annual bonuses, job classifications, and health and safety. As elsewhere, the gains that were won in Italy, including an increase in pay for the night shift at MXP5 Piacenza, stronger contestation over the pace of work, and improvements to PPE in the early stages of the COVID-19 pandemic, were centrally reliant on growing confidence and organization among workers.[15] As presented in Chapter 4, Amazon's behaviour during the access period prior to the 2024 BHX4 recognition ballot severely impeded real contact with workers even when a formal right to access was in place – including close surveillance, shadowing and control over the movements of organizers and restriction on when workers could speak to organizers or worker-leaders, and the communication worker-leaders could have with their colleagues. As discussed in Chapters 3 and 5, the spatial and social organization of the workplace and recruitment and promotion practices can also create obstacles to access. These issues should be taken into account as part of the further development and implementation of legislation. Whatever the changes to the law, no doubt many issues will remain to be contested and worked out in practice between unions and employers in the course of establishing the terms of specific access agreements. This highlights the enduring importance of the principles, strategies and tactics discussed in this book to the contested times and spaces of work and trade unionism.

By way of a final summary

For unions: a sustained and well-resourced commitment to listening to workers and identifying and developing leaders among precarious and highly diverse workforces can produce tangible gains in recruitment and material wins for members, together with long-term development of new leaders.

For scholars and students: political content is more important than organizational form in building communities of struggle among precarious workers, the age and size of traditional trade unions does not present an insurmountable barrier to agility where there is sufficient decentralization, and larger unions' financial resources can be a great benefit in creating spaces and times for precarious workers to organize.

Notes

[1] Però, D. (2020) 'Indie unions, organising and labour renewal: learning from precarious migrant workers', *Work, Employment and Society*, 34(5): 900–918.

[2] Little, G., Sharp, E., Stevenson, H. and Wilson, D. (2023) *Lessons in Organising: What Trade Unionists Can Learn from the War on Teachers*, London: Pluto.

[3] Vickers, T. (2019) *Borders, Migration and Class: Producing Immigrants and Workers*, Bristol: Bristol University Press.

[4] McAlevey, J.F. (2016) *No Shortcuts: Organizing for Power*, Oxford: Oxford University Press, p 188.

[5] McAlevey (n 5), p 28.

[6] McBride, J., Stirling, J. and Winter, S. (2013) ' "Because we were living it": the hidden work of a strike', *Work, Employment and Society*, 27(2): 244–253.

[7] Allinson, I. (2022) *Workers Can Win: A Guide to Organising at Work*, London: Pluto Press, p 150.

[8] Holgate, J. (2015) 'An international study of trade union involvement in community organising: same model, different outcomes', *British Journal of Industrial Relations*', 53(2): 460–483, at 463; see also Schmidt, E. (2005) 'Coalition building: trade union dialogues with civil society', *Transfer*, 11(3): 449–456.

[9] Boyle, K. A. (2024) 'The Discursive power of trade union leadership: framing identity fields for public persuasion', *Work, Employment and Society*, DOI:10.1177/09500170241279778.

[10] Vickers, T. (2019) *Borders, Migration and Class: Producing Immigrants and Workers*, Bristol: Bristol University Press.

[11] Olney, P. and Wilson, R. (2020) 'Think big: organising a successful Amazon workers' movement in the United States by combining the strengths of the left and organised labor', in J. Alimahomed-Wilson and E. Reese (eds) *The Cost of Free Shipping: Amazon in the Global Economy*, London: Pluto Press, pp 250–264.

[12] Holgate, J. (2021) *Arise: Power, Strategy and Union Resurgence*, London: Pluto Press; Little, G., Sharp, E., Stevenson, H. and Wilson, D. (2023) *Lessons in Organising: What Trade Unionists Can Learn from the War on Teachers*, London: Pluto Press.

[13] Però, D. (2020) 'Indie unions, organising and labour renewal: learning from precarious migrant workers', *Work, Employment and Society*, 34(5): 900–918, at 901.

[14] Massimo, F. (2020) 'A struggle for bodies and souls: Amazon management and union strategies in France and Italy', in J. Alimahomed-Wilson and E. Reese (eds) *The Cost of Free Shipping: Amazon in the Global Economy*, London: Pluto Press, pp 129–144.

[15] Delfanti, A. (2021) *The Warehouse: Workers and Robots at Amazon*, London: Pluto Press, pp 12, 47.

APPENDIX 1

Case Study Questions for Teaching

1. What were the main issues of concern among BHX4 workers?
2. Can you identify issues that were more of a priority for some BHX4 workers than others?
3. How did Amazon and the GMB respond to different issues, considering those issues that only affected some workers and those that were widely felt across the workforce?
4. What mechanisms did Amazon make available for worker voice at BHX4 and how effective were these?
5. How was worker voice at BHX4 affected by:
   a. organization of the labour process;
   b. management style;
   c. recruitment and promotion;
   d. managers' attitude towards trade unions?
6. What role did HR play in this case study?
7. How did the GMB Union approach each of the following challenges at BHX:
   a. reaching the whole workforce;
   b. sustaining action and engagement;
   c. developing leadership;
   d. responding to workers' needs and concerns;
   e. building wider support.
8. Imagine you were either a worker-leader, a GMB organizer, a manager or HR at each of the following critical moments. Would you have done anything differently and why?

   a. August 2022 pay rise;
   b. first application for CAC recognition;
   c. second application for CAC recognition;
   d. November 2024 pay rise.
9. List all of the ways in which state regulations played a role in this case.
10. For each aspect of state regulation you have listed, consider how this might change, and then what do you predict that the consequence of this change would be?
11. List all the other stakeholders you can think of that are affected in some way by this case. For each of these, consider in what way they are affected.

APPENDIX 2

Methodology:
An Activist Ethnography

I undertook the bulk of the research that informs this book during a part-time secondment to the GMB Union between January and July 2024, funded by Nottingham Trent University. GMB organizers requested my assistance in documenting their campaign at Amazon's BHX4 site because they were receiving many questions and requests to share their approach with other organizers, but were too busy organizing to document this themselves. The resulting research took the form of an activist ethnography, drawing on Reedy and King's concept of 'friendship as method'.[1] This involved me taking an explicit and open position of solidarity with the GMB workers and foregrounding the seldom-heard and often-marginalized perspectives of worker-leaders and frontline union organizers, contributing to what Sandra Harding calls 'strong objectivity', which, to be fully realized, must be accompanied by a 'strong reflexivity' and a 'strong method'.[2] Consistent with this methodology, I was at the same time an academic researcher and an active participant in GMB organizing work, for example, helping to distribute union literature on picket lines, informing the union on matters of immigration policy, and brokering relationships with community, migrant and legal advice organizations. Holgate discusses the pros and cons of such 'insider-outsider' research with trade unions, with benefits for access and understandings produced through membership of the 'epistemic community' that is being studied, but cautions that in order to maintain academic rigour, the beliefs and behaviour of the researcher should be opened up to scrutiny and participants should be provided with opportunities to comment on findings prior to publication;[3] these measures have been implemented throughout.

My participation was combined with direct observation and interviews, producing data that were used to conduct a strengths-based analysis of the GMB's organizing practice.[4] This analysis aimed to help the union to identify those aspects of its practice that made the greatest contribution in tackling the challenges faced by workers in organizing at BHX4, to reflect on how these strengths might be further developed and to identify transferable lessons for future campaigns. This analysis was co-produced with the active and regular involvement of GMB organizers and worker-leaders, in particular Tom Rigby, who chairs national meetings of the GMB's Regional Education Officers and is thus well informed about strengths and training needs across the union.

Data included fieldnotes from direct observations of nine strike pickets and six mass strike meetings, alongside nine training sessions for worker-leaders, numerous other meetings, WhatsApp group discussions, and informal conversations with approximately 200 workers, in order to understand the organizing process in context and including the complex and dynamic social relations at play. In-depth semi-structured interviews were conducted with 11 leaders among the Amazon workers and four GMB organizers, supplemented by an extended written submission by another worker-leader, to access their interpretations of the organizing process and recollections of past events. Of the 16 people who contributed in this way, five were women and 11 were men, and ten were from a Global Majority background. Specific countries of origin for participants are not named in order to protect anonymity.

Informed consent was given verbally and in writing by all interviewees, consistent with the British Sociological Association 2017 Statement of Ethical Practice, and the project received a positive assessment by an ethics committee at Nottingham Trent University. I emphasized to interviewees that they did not have to answer any question that they did not wish to, and gave them the opportunity to withdraw their data up to a specified date. Data was anonymized to protect individuals' identities and participants are referred to using reference codes, specifying only whether an individual is a worker-leader or an organizer, and whether they are from a Global Majority or European background, withholding other demographic information that might risk individuals being identified. Where a worker is European but also a migrant, this is noted because of the differential position of stigma and rights associated with migration.[5]

Interview transcripts and fieldnotes were analysed thematically, drawing on Miles and Huberman.[6] I developed an inductive coding framework in discussion with Tom Rigby and a worker-leader; this was trialled at two conferences, where I received feedback that confirmed the effectiveness of this framework in terms of drawing lessons for other contexts. This analysis was also informed by my own experience of two decades of organizing in migrant rights, housing, international solidarity and employment campaigns, including several years as a rep and branch committee member for the University and College Union (UCU). The analytical framework produced through this process aimed to capture the union's responses to five areas of challenge that emerged from interviews and fieldwork observations as important in terms of shaping unionization at BHX4:

- reaching the whole workforce;
- sustaining action and engagement;
- developing leadership;
- responding to members' needs and concerns;
- building wider support.

Within these themes, a total of 24 challenges and 24 responses were identified (see Appendix 3 for details). Detailed coding of the transcripts and fieldnotes was then conducted, the results of which are presented in Chapters 3–7. From this, a set of core principles constituting the 'Coventry Model' was developed in collaboration with Tom Rigby and piloted as part of an event to share learning between organizers and worker-leaders from the GMB's Midlands and North East, Yorkshire and Humber regions. These principles were then substantially revised, again in close collaboration with Tom Rigby, to focus on the most distinctive lessons learned through the BHX4 struggle. These lessons focused on using and creating and times and spaces for worker organizing in contexts that are highly controlled by the employer and have little or no permitted access for unions. A final draft of the book was shared with all interviewees and with Amazon in written and audio formats, accompanied by a two-page summary of its central arguments and conclusions, as a final check for internal validity and opportunity for comment.

Throughout this book, my research findings are interspersed with essays by worker-leaders and organizers. Dillon characterizes the essay form as diverse in expression, aiming for the essence of a subject without pretending to be exhaustive, and remaining personal and therefore partial in its coverage and rooted to a particular time and place.[7] It is therefore well suited to expressing the views of organizers and worker-leaders that are deeply felt and grounded in each person's experience of the collective processes of work and organizing. These essays add to the text by bringing the reader into direct contact with the voices of leading figures in the unionization process, with less mediation than occurs through the more conventional academic presentation of short quotations from interviews. This can be seen as a form of 'workers inquiry',[8] informed by a recognition that there are aspects of the work process – including trade union organizing, which can be seen as a form of work or practice – that can only be properly understood and represented by workers themselves, in tandem with the recognition that only workers can liberate themselves. As was further explained in Chapter 5, the worker-leaders who contributed these essays were selected for their leadership role through an extensive process of nomination by their colleagues, and their perspectives therefore represent leading ideas, experiences and reflections among the more than 1,400 workers who make up the GMB Union inside BHX4. Alongside these, the essays by GMB organizers interpret their experience at BHX4 in the context of other campaigns across multiple settings, in some cases encompassing decades of experience. I formulated essay topics to unpick key issues that had arisen in conversation with these individuals and on which I felt they were ideally placed to comment. All essay authors were offered the opportunity to select a different topic, but none did so. All authors were given the opportunity to remain anonymous, but all chose to be named. I edited these essays with the aim of bringing out each distinctive voice. All edits were approved by that essay's author.

Notes
[1] Reedy, P.C. and King, D.R. (2019) 'Critical performativity in the field: methodological principles for activist ethnographers', *Organizational Research Methods*, 22(2): 564–589.

[2] Hirsh, E. and Olson, G.A. (1995) 'Starting from marginalized lives: a conversation with Sandra Harding', *JAC*, 15(2): 193–225.

[3] Holgate, J. (2021b) 'Trade unions in the community: building broad spaces of solidarity', *Economic and Industrial Democracy*, 42(2): 226–247, at 234.

[4] Bushe, G. R. (2011) 'Appreciative inquiry: theory and critique', in D. Boje, B. Burnes and J. Hassard (eds) *The Routledge Companion to Organizational Change*, Abingdon: Routledge, pp 87–103.

[5] Blachnicka-Ciacek, D. and Budginaite-Mackine, I. (2022) 'The ambiguous lives of "the other whites": class and racialisation of Eastern European migrants in the UK', *Sociological Review*, 70(6): 1081–1099.

[6] Miles, M.B. and Huberman, A.M. (2014) *Qualitative Data Analysis: A Methods Sourcebook*, Thousand Oaks: Sage.

[7] Dillon, B. (2017). *Essayism*, London: Fitzcarraldo Editions, pp 18–19.

[8] Woodcock, J. (2014) 'The workers' inquiry from Trotskyism to Operaismo: a political methodology for investigating the workplace', *Ephemera: Theory and Politics in Organisation*, 14(3): 489–509.

APPENDIX 3

Coding Framework

1. Reaching the whole workforce
   Challenges:
   - 1c1. Highly controlled work environment
   - 1c2. Massive scale divided by shifts and departments and contract types
   - 1c3. Many different nationalities and languages
   - 1c4. Long working hours
   - 1c5. High turnover in staff
   - 1c6. People live far away and travel in

   Responses:
   - 1r1. Laying the foundations
   - 1r2. Seizing the time
   - 1r3. Leading with strikes protesting substantive issues – recruiting on the picket line and after
   - 1r4. Making use of Amazon's own structures – VOA Board, Associate Forum, Team Connects, All Hands Meetings

2. Sustaining action and engagement
   Challenges:
   - 2c1. Fear of victimization and anti-union propaganda
   - 2c2. Vulnerabilities due to immigration status
   - 2c3. Families reliant on remittances
   - 2c4. Knowledge of UK laws and institutions

   Responses:
   - 2r1. Enabling strike action with hardship payments while maintaining accountability

2r2. Winning ballots with a growing membership – gate jobs, phone banking, peer-to-peer texting, translation, scholarships, orange envelopes

2r3. Applying for recognition within the limitations of the CAC process, supported by legal challenges with Foxglove, CAC reform with LP

2r4. Offering members representation and protection

3. Developing leadership

Challenges:

3c1. Amazon targets specific communities

3c2. Promotion practices encourage division

3c3. Little trade union experience

3c4. Officers from different backgrounds

3c5. Attempts by Amazon to pressure or buy off leaders and present GMB as an alien 'business'

Responses:

3r1. Sharing leadership within the union and across usual teams, willingness to try new things and take ideas on board

3r2. Strikes and strike schools as a forum for mapping and to frame the union's messaging

3r3. Strikes as an environment to build relationships and identify and develop leaders – active picketing as contestation and celebration

3r4. Developing leaders across different communities – nomination and weekly training-strategy meetings

3r5. Identifying wins

3r6. Articulating injuries and deepening knowledge of rights

3r7. Supporting leaders to weather the storm of Amazon harassment, support from officers, MPs, media, mass meetings, WhatsApp

4. Responding to members' concerns

Challenges:

4c1. Immigration and visa concerns

4c2. English language

4c3. Housing

4c4. Health

4c5. Family

Responses:

4r1. The importance of informal conversations

4r2. Recognizing wider issues as part of union business, expression in 'GMB Family'

4r3. Working creatively to expand the union's understanding and capacity – for example, ESOL, immigration advice, meetings with other organizations

4r4. Organizing, not mobilizing

5. Building wider support

Challenges:

5c1. Important source of fundraising to supplement strike fund through union branch donations

5c2. Social dependency on Amazon

5c3. Low level of social movement activity

Responses:

5r1. Amazon Workers Support Group

5r2. TUC campaigning

5r3. Campaigning to change government policy – procurement, CAC and so on

5r4. International coalition building

Index

References to notes show both the page number and the note number (95n1).